THE ROUGH GUIDE to the

iPhone

Peter Buckley
& Duncan Clark

ROUGH
GUIDES

www.roughguides.com

Credits

The Rough Guide to the iPhone

Text, design and layout:
Peter Buckley and Duncan Clark
Proofreading: Diane Margolis
Production: Rebecca Short

Rough Guides Reference

Series editor: Mark Ellingham
Editors: Peter Buckley, Duncan Clark,
Tracy Hopkins, Sean Mahoney,
Matt Milton, Joe Staines, Ruth Tidball
Director: Andrew Lockett

Apple hardware images courtesy of Apple UK

Acknowledgements

The authors would like to thank everyone at Rough Guides, above all Sean Mahoney, who
gallantly stood in line for 14 hours on the day of the iPhone's launch to secure the hardware
used to write this book, and also provided very useful comments on the manuscript. Also
Andrew Lockett and John Duhigg, for signing up the project in record time.

Publishing information

This first edition published September 2007 by Rough Guides Ltd:
80 Strand, London WC2R 0RL
345 Hudson St, 4th Floor, New York 10014, USA
mail@roughguides.com

Distributed by the Penguin Group:
Penguin Books Ltd, 80 Strand, London WC2R 0RL
Penguin Putnam, Inc., 375 Hudson Street, NY 10014, USA
Penguin Group (Australia), 250 Camberwell Road, Camberwell, Victoria 3124, Australia
Penguin Books Canada Ltd, 10 Alcorn Avenue, Toronto, Ontario, M4P 2Y3, Canada
Penguin Group (New Zealand), 67 Apollo Drive, Mairangi Bay, Auckland 1310, New Zealand

Typeset in Minion and Myriad

ISBN 13: 978-1-84353-924-7
ISBN 10: 1-84353-924-1

1 3 5 7 9 8 6 4 2

Contents

Introduction

The iPhone was probably the most keenly anticipated consumer product of all time. After years of rumours, predictions and discussions, Apple finally previewed the device in early 2007. That was six months before the iPhone went on sale in the US and nearly a year before it would be available in Europe, but photos of the gadget were nonetheless all over newspaper front pages around the world the following morning. It was the sort of media coverage that no other company could even have dreamed of. But then no other company had created the iPod.

In the months after the preview, traders sold iPhone Web addresses on eBay for huge sums, accessory manufacturers scrambled to produce add-ons for a device they'd never actually seen, and bloggers dissected Steve Job's presentation in minute detail for clues about what the iPhone would or wouldn't be able to do.

By the time the phone actually went on sale, things had reached fever pitch. Apple and AT&T stores across the US saw lines of early adopters camping on the streets to ensure that they wouldn't miss out on release day and have to wait a couple of weeks for restocks. Savvy students hired themselves out as line-standers, and websites pointed iPhone campers in the direction of the most conveniently located toilets, restaurants and DVD rental stores.

That was the Friday. By the end of the weekend, more than half a million phones had been sold, with another half-million or so flying off the shelves the following week. By any account, Apple had scored a major success.

But was all the excitement justified? Not according to some commentators, who described the whole scene as an example of mass hysteria – a triumph of PR spin. Phones that do email, music and Web browsing have existed for years, they pointed out, and many of them offer greater functionality or a broader feature array than the iPhone. And at a lower price, too.

But that's to miss the point. There have indeed been many smart phones released over the years, but they've consistently been ugly, fiddly, unintuitive and unergonomic. They look and feel like they were designed by people who are interested in "functionality" and "feature arrays" rather than whether a device is actually pleasurable to use – people who create "solutions" rather than products. Such phones have always been aimed primarily at businesses and have names reminiscent of the corporate computer systems they're designed to work with – the Motorola MC70, for instance, or Palm Treo 700WX.

By comparison, the iPhone is nicely designed, simple to use, and does what you actually want it to do. Its innovations are not in its "feature array" but in its human interface – a screen that lets you easily flick through long lists of contacts or zoom in on a webpage with the touch of a finger or two; a sensor that lets you rotate the device to make a horizontal picture fills the screen; a button that takes you back to the Home screen, from where you can access every application with one tap.

Once people had seen these features in action, the hype was generated from the bottom up. All Apple did was put out a few ads – there was no guerilla marketing campaign or PR offensive.

(Indeed, as all technology journalists know, it's almost impossible to get through to Apple PR, let alone get someone to return your call.)

That's not to say that the iPhone is beyond criticism. It has its faults and limitations, of course. And you could make a reasonable case that so much buzz over a mobile phone, however pretty and ergonomic it may be, is an example of rampant, unsustainable consumerism – a focus on expensive toys in an era of conflict and climate change.

That may well be, but mobile phones are here to stay. And if we're going to have them, we may as well have ones that are good to use, long-lasting and include iPod functions, so that we don't end up buying and carrying around multiple devices. The iPhone checks all of these boxes, and plenty more besides.

Whether you're thinking about buying an iPhone or you already have one, this is the book to have. It covers the whole topic, from questions you might want answering before you buy, and advice on importing numbers from an old handset, through to advanced tips for getting the iPhone to do things that it currently can't do straight out of the box – such as act as a hard drive or open a Web link into a new window.

We've even included, towards the back of the book, some samples of the spoofs and other weird and wonderful online creations that the iPhone phenomenon has brought about. However much of an iPhone addict you become, it's good to know that some people are even more obsessed…

Primer

01 iPhone Q&A

Everything you ever wanted to know but were afraid to ask

The big picture

What's an iPhone?

An iPhone is a smart phone – that is, a mobile telephone that offers extra features such as Web browsing and email as well as music and video playback. The device is produced by Apple, manufacturers of the iPod and Mac computers.

After years of speculation, and to great media fanfare, the iPhone was launched in the US on June 29, 2007. It will go on sale in other countries throughout 2007 and 2008.

How does it compare to other smart phones?

There are loads of smart phones on the market, many of which offer a similar feature list to that of the iPhone, including Web

browsing, email, and music and video playback. The main difference is that the iPhone is (generally) a pleasure to use, whereas
most other smart phones are fiddly and confusing.

Some of the relative advantages of the iPhone, besides its slick
design, are:

▶ A huge, bright, high-
resolution screen that changes
orientation when you rotate
the phone

▶ A flexible touch-screen
interface instead of a fixed
keyboard

▶ An extremely user-friendly
software system

▶ Gigabytes of storage space

▶ An excellent, easy-to-use
Web browser

▶ Compatibility with iTunes

▶ Wi-Fi capability for
connecting to wireless
networks

▶ Visual Voicemail, whereby
you can see voicemails in an
inbox-style list and listen to
them in any order you like

That's not to say that the iPhone is perfect. Apple have missed out
quite a few features (see box), and a few elements of the interface
and software may annoy some users.

A few things the iPhone can't do (yet)

Following are some things which the first-generation iPhone cannot do – at least not at the time of launch. Software updates could add nearly all of these features and functions in the future.

▶ **Picture and video messaging** Though you can email a photo.

▶ **Voice dialling** You can only make a call by tapping the screen.

▶ **Voice memos** The closest equivalent would be leaving yourself a voicemail.

▶ **Video capture** You can take pictures but not video clips.

▶ **Call recording** You can't tap calls, spy-style.

▶ **Hard-drive mode** Though there is a third-party Mac application that adds this feature (see p.210).

▶ **Zoom in when taking photos** But you can zoom in on the resulting pictures.

▶ **Play iPod games** downloaded from iTunes. There are, however, lots of games online (see p.228).

▶ **Play through a TV** Unlike video iPods, there's no TV-out signal.

▶ **Copy & paste text** But you can email notes and URLs.

▶ **Songs or custom ringtones** You have to stick with the pre-installed ringtones.

▶ **Undo** your last action.

▶ **Receive radio** – either Internet streams, DAB or FM.

▶ **Flash, Java, RSS, RealPlayer or Windows Media** Items within webpages that rely on these technologies won't display.

▶ **Talk to printers, keyboards, mice, computers or other phones via Bluetooth** You can only connect to headsets and carphone systems.

▶ **Chat** You can SMS but not chat in realtime – except via the Web (see p.108).

▶ **Edit documents** You can read and forward PDFs, Word and Excel docs, but not edit them.

▶ **Run Skype** Though there are similar services that you can operate via Safari (see p.103).

▶ **Deliver stereo sound** via a Bluetooth headset.

▶ **GPS (Global Positioning System)** You can view maps, but the phone won't automatically know exactly where you are.

▶ **Make calls accidentally by knocking buttons in a bag** since the iPhone only responds to fingers.

How does the iPhone compare to the iPod?

The iPhone *is* an iPod, in addition to being a phone and an Internet device. It can do nearly everything a normal iPod can do – such as playing music, videos and podcasts – and offers a couple of new tools, such as the "Cover Flow" view for browsing music by album artwork (see p.138).

The main advantage of a traditional iPod is storage space. The first-generation iPhones offer 4 or 8 gigabytes of space, while the fifth-generation iPod offers up to 80 gigabytes.

How does it compare to a computer for Web browsing and email?

No pocket-sized Internet device can match a computer with large screen, mouse and a full-sized keyboard, but the iPhone comes about as close as you could hope. Web browsing, in particular, is very well handled, with a great interface for zooming in and out on sections of a webpage. However, when you're out and about, you'll find the access very slow compared to a home broadband connection. (More on this later.)

The email tool is slightly less impressive. It does everything you need it to do, but is annoying in some ways. For example, deleting multiple messages is a bit cumbersome, there's no BCC field, and it doesn't copy your Sent messages over to the email application on your Mac or PC. These annoyances may be fixed in future software updates.

Can I use an iPhone as a hard drive to move files between computers?

No, not at present. Unlike the iPod, the iPhone doesn't offer a "disk mode" to allow storage of any computer files. The most likely reason for this is that using the device as a hard drive would require you to "eject" it from your computer before disconnecting, which would be a real pain if you had an incoming call. There is, however, a software work-around for Macs (see p.210).

What else can it do?

In addition to those features already mentioned, the iPhone comes with a very useful maps application and easy-to-use weather and stock tools, plus good versions of standard fare such as a calculator, alarm clock and notes. For more on these applications, see p.199.

Can't it edit Word and Excel docs?

For now, no. You can open, read and forward Word and Excel docs sent to you by email, but you can't edit them. Again, this may change in the future, but Apple has so far made no promises to that effect.

The bigger picture is that Apple has decided to keep the iPhone as a "closed platform", meaning that it will only run a handful of applications produced by Apple themselves. The stated reason for this is that imperfect programs could cause the phone to crash or become buggy. Apple would rather the phone did some things well and reliably, rather than lots of things badly and unreliably.

Many programmers found this announcement frustrating, since they'd been looking forward to creating applications for the phone ever since the earlier announcement that it would run OS X.

What's OS X?

All computers have an operating system – underlying software that acts as a bridge between the hardware, the user and the applications. The standard operating system on PCs is Windows; on Macs, it's OS X.

The iPhone, then, shares its fundamental software with Mac computers, but you wouldn't know it, since the version of OS X on the iPhone is slimmed down and has a different look and feel – a "front end" specially designed to make the most of the phone's touch-screen interface.

Is the on-screen keyboard easy to use?

Apple are very proud of the iPhone's touch-screen keyboard and the accompanying error-correcting software that aims to minimize typos. In general, reviewers and owners alike have been pleasantly surprised at how quickly they've got used to it. Inevitably, however, it's not to everyone's taste.

When you're using the Web browser – though not other applications – you can rotate the iPhone through ninety degrees to use a bigger version of the keyboard in landscape mode.

Can you operate the iPhone with one hand?

Yes, this is perfectly possible: your fingers hold the body of the device and your thumb can access the screen. However, typing is much faster with two hands.

Will the touch screen work with gloves on?

No – at least not in our experiments. Unless, of course, you wear fingerless gloves. But then most modern mobiles are at best fiddly with a pair of gloves. The iPhone also won't work with a stylus or connect to a mouse.

Do I need a computer to use an iPhone?

Yes – or at the very least you need access to one. You can't activate an iPhone without a Mac or PC. Moreover, a computer is the only way to get music, video and other media onto the phone. To copy a CD onto an iPhone, for example, you first copy it onto the computer and then transfer it from computer to phone. Likewise if you want to download songs and movies from the Internet: the iPhone can't access the iTunes Store directly, so you have to use a computer to purchase your downloads.

One advantage of this way of working is that you don't lose any data if you lose the iPhone – everything is safely duplicated on your Mac or PC.

Is my current computer up to the job?

If you bought a PC or Mac in the last few years, it will probably be capable of working with an iPhone, but it's certainly worth checking before spending any money. The box overleaf explains the minimum requirements and the upgrade options if your computer doesn't have what it takes.

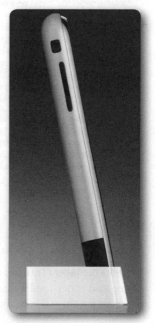

How does the phone connect to the computer?

With a USB2 cable either connected directly to the iPhone or to a Dock (pictured) into which the iPhone slots. The phone can't talk to the computer wirelessly.

Computer requirements & upgrade options

According to Apple, to use an iPhone you need a computer that meets the following minimum requirements:

Mac: OS X 10.4.10 and a USB2 port
PC: Windows Vista or XP and a USB2 port

Nearly all Macs and PCs produced since mid-2005, including laptops, should fulfil these criteria, and some older ones will also work. But it's worth checking your hardware and software before shelling out. Here's how:

Checking your version of Windows
To check your operating system on a PC, right-click the My Computer icon and select Properties. If you don't have Windows Vista or XP, you probably have Windows Me or 98. You could consider upgrading, but you'll have to pay (around $95/£85); it can be a bit of a headache (some older programs and hardware won't work on XP or Vista); and you'll need to check whether your hardware is up to the job (see microsoft.com for more details). If you have Windows 95, it's probably a matter of buying a new computer.
   Note that the 64-bit version of Windows Vista isn't supported by the iPhone at the time of launch. (If you don't know what that means, fear not – you won't have the 64-bit version.) Also note that, if you have an older copy of Windows XP, you may need to run Windows Update to install the Service Pack 2 update before your computer will work with an iPhone.

Checking your version of Mac OS X
On a Mac, select About This Mac or System Profiler from the Apple menu in the top-left corner of the screen. If the OS X number starts with 10.4 or 10.5, you'll be fine, though you might have to run the Software Update tool (also in the Apple menu) to grab the latest updates.

What's iTunes?

iTunes is a piece of software produced by Apple for Macs and PCs. It serves four main functions:

▶ **Media manager** iTunes is used for managing and playing music, video and other media on a Mac or PC. This includes everything from importing CDs to making playlists.

If you have OS X 10.3 or earlier, the iPhone won't work; you'll have to upgrade to the latest version of OS X, which will cost you around $130/£90. But first check the hardware requirements to make sure your machine can handle the newer operating system (see apple.com/macosx) and also check whether you have a USB2 socket (see below). You may find that you'd be better off buying a new Mac.

USB2 port

This is the port (socket) to which you connect the iPhone. Any USB socket will work, but data transfer to the phone will be painfully slow unless you have a USB2 socket, which is why Apple specify USB2 as a minimum requirement. USB2 sockets are found on most PCs and Macs made after 2003; to be sure, check your computer's manual, as USB and USB2 ports look identical.

If you don't have a USB2 port, you could add one to your computer by purchasing a suitable adapter. These are available for as little as $30/£20 for desktops and around double that for laptops. Or, if you have the right port but it's usually occupied by another device, buy a powered "hub" to turn a single port into two or more. These start at around $30/£20.

iPhones work fine with laptops as well as desktops, and PCs as well as Macs

▶ **iPhone and iPod manager** iTunes is the program that is used for copying music, movies, photos and other data from a computer to an iPhone or iPod.

▶ **Download store** The iTunes Store is Apple's legal, pay-to-use music and video download service. It can only be reached via iTunes – not via a Web browser.

▶ **Podcast aggregator** You can use iTunes to subscribe for free to hundreds of audio or video podcasts for use on your computer, iPhone or iPod.

What's all the controversy about the battery?

Like the original iPods, the iPhone has received quite a lot of negative publicity over its battery, which gradually dies over time and can only be replaced by Apple for a substantial fee ($76 in the US).

To be fair, *all* rechargeable batteries deteriorate over time and eventually die. The only difference with iPhones is that the replacements cost more than for other phones – and that you can't fit them yourself (at least not in theory). The high cost can partly be explained by the nature of the battery. Few pocket devices offer hours of video playback or such large, bright screens. That type of performance is comparable to a laptop – and laptop batteries are even more expensive. As for sending the device back to Apple, this is irritating, for sure, though at least it means that the device can be properly sealed and free from the flimsy battery flaps that often get broken on other phones.

Though Apple don't recommend it, it has long been possible to source bargain iPod batteries on the Internet and fit them yourself, or pay someone else to do it. It's probably fair to assume that the same will turn out to be true for the iPhone, too.

As for the longevity of the battery, expect to replace it after 2–4 years, depending on how much you drain it each day. For more information about the battery, see p.68.

Does the iPhone contain a hard drive?

No. Like the iPod nano and shuffle, the iPhone stores its information on so-called flash memory: tiny chips of the kind found in digital-camera memory cards. These have a smaller capacity than hard drives, but they're less bulky, less power hungry and less likely to break if the device is dropped.

Does the screen scratch easily?

It's not invulnerable, but the iPhone screen is significantly more scratch resistant than that of an iPod. In our tests, a few weeks of carrying an iPhone around in a pocket with keys and coins resulted in no visible scratches.

Does the iPhone present any security risks?

Not really. There's a theoretical risk with any smart phone that someone could "hack" it remotely and access any stored information. But the risk is extremely small – especially in the case of the iPhone which, by default, won't allow Bluetooth access from laptops or other phones. The only substantial risk is that someone could steal your phone and access private data or make expensive long-distance calls on your account. If you're worried about that possibility, the best defence is to password-protect your iPhone – see p.55 to find out how.

Phone issues

If I get an iPhone, do I have to change carrier and get a new contract?

Maybe. The iPhone is available exclusively on AT&T in the US and won't work on any other network. The same situation is expected in other countries – including the UK, where O2 looks set to be the partner carrier.

In the US, if you're already with AT&T, you can simply add an unlimited data plan (for Web browsing and email) to your existing

Locked in with another carrier?

If you're locked into a contract with a phone company that doesn't offer the iPhone, there are various things you could try in order to excuse yourself from the get-out fee. Soon after the iPhone's launch, Wired.com's Daniel Dumas listed a whole host of ideas, from faking your own death to being deployed abroad for military service. Here are a few of his more realistic suggestions:

▶ **Hand on your contract** Use a website such as CellTradeUSA.com to find someone willing to take your plan off your hands.

▶ **Move out of range** Tell your phone company that you're moving to an area that their network doesn't cover and they may be happy to terminate the contract.

▶ **Beat them at their own game** Check your original contract to see whether it would be rendered void by small changes they've already made, such as giving you extra minutes or text messages.

▶ **Ask to see the contract** The carrier should be able to show you the contract that you signed. If they can't – or they simply can't be bothered to dig it out from their records office – that may give you grounds to walk.

voice plan at a cost of $20 per month. If you're with another carrier, you'll need to leave your existing network and sign up with AT&T. If you're tied in to your existing contract for a set period of time, this might mean paying a get-out fee. Ask your current carrier for details (or see the above box for some other options).

Either way, you'll get to keep your current phone number; transferring the number is part of the activation process.

Can I not just use the SIM card from my current phone and stick with my current network?

Theoretically not. You can swap the SIMs between two iPhones, but if you insert a non-approved SIM from a different phone, you'll get an error message and it won't work. Within hours of the iPhone being launched, geeks across America were working to find a way to "unlock" the phone and get around this. If and when they succeed, this will make it possible to use the iPhone on almost any network and in almost any country – but only for those people who don't mind invalidating their warranty by updating the phone with non-Apple-approved software. For more information on the state of play, see:

iPhone Hacks iphonehacks.com
iPhoneUnlocking iphoneunlocking.com

Do I really need to sign a two-year contract? What about prepaid / pay-as-you-go?

In the US, new AT&T customers have to enter into a two-year contract as part of the process of activating their iPhone. Though Apple have never widely publicized the fact, there is an alternative option – a prepaid plan that offers fewer minutes but doesn't tie you in for a set period. A sample plan at the time of writing is $60 per month for 300 minutes, 1000 night and evening minutes, and unlimited data and voicemail.

The prepaid option is made available during purchase or activation only to those who are deemed to have a bad credit rating. However, some bloggers with good credit ratings claim to have successfully signed up by entering a social security number of 999-99-9999 during activation.

It remains to be seen how the contracts will work in the UK and other countries.

Can I use the iPhone overseas?

Yes, the iPhone is quad-band so will work for voice calls in nearly 200 countries, the most prominent exceptions being Japan and South Korea, whose networks generally require 3G-compatible handsets. However, you'll need to be prepared to pay some rather steep call charges (see box overleaf).

Before leaving your home country, you may first need to activate international roaming on your account. This shouldn't be difficult – American iPhone owners can call AT&T on 1-800-331-0500 – though it might be subject to your credit rating or payment history with the carrier in question.

To avoid roaming charges, you could consider trying to get your iPhone unlocked (see p.22), which would allow you to use it with a local pay-as-you-go SIM card from the country you're visiting. This might save you cash, but unlocking, if it even works, presents various problems, as already discussed. Moreover, when a foreign

Sample AT&T roaming charges

These are the fees levied on US AT&T customers using their phones abroad. For a full list of World Travel costs, visit AT&T.com

	Standard rate	World Traveler rate ($5.99 per month)
Calls		
Mexico	$0.99	$0.59
France, Greece, Iceland, Italy Germany, Spain, UK	$1.29	$0.99
Jamaica, Barbados, T&T	$1.99	$1.69
Brazil, Argentina, Colombia China, Turkey	$2.29	$1.99
South Africa, India, Egypt,	$2.49	$1.69–2.49
Russia, Mali, Ukraine, Vietnam	$3–5	$2–5
Messages		
Charges only applied for sending, not receiving		
Text messages	$0.50	$0.50
Data use		
Internet/email	$19.50 per megabyte of data	

SIM is in place, you won't be able to receive calls to your usual number. All told, if you travel to one country a lot, it might be simpler to buy an inexpensive prepaid phone in that country and arrange to have calls to your regular iPhone number forwarded (see p.102).

Note that, when travelling overseas, you may not be able to access Visual Voicemail, Instead, voicemail will work in the old-fashioned way.

Will I be able to get the contact numbers off my old phone and onto the iPhone?

In general, yes, but the process depends on your old phone and your computer. See p.78 for more information.

Internet issues

Does the iPhone offer fast Internet access?

Yes and no. On the move, current iPhones offer relatively slow Internet access, which isn't helped by the fact that they use EDGE rather than 3G. But the iPhone can offer broadband speeds when connected via Wi-Fi (read on to find out what this means in English). Even here, however, it won't be as fast as the same connection accessed via a Mac or PC.

EGDE, 3G … what's all that about?

Over time, the technology used to transmit and receive calls and data from mobile phones has improved, allowing greater range and speed. Of the network technologies widely available at present, 3G (third generation) is the most advanced, allowing Internet access at speeds comparable to home broadband connections.

Much to the surprise of many commentators, the first-generation iPhone doesn't access the Internet via 3G. Instead, it uses a network known as EDGE (Enhanced Data rates for GSM Evolution, to give it its rather grand full name). According to Apple, the main reasons for this decision were that EDGE is more widely available in non-urban areas than 3G, and that EGDE-based phones offer better battery life.

EDGE, which is usually referred to as "2.75G", offers a theoretical top speed of 236 kilobits per second (kbps); in practice, however, users have more often than not experienced connections as slow as 50kbps – like an old-fashioned dial-up connection. Thankfully, things have recently improved a little.

When David Pogue reviewed the iPhone for the *New York Times* in June 2007, a few days before its launch, he reported painfully slow speeds for mobile browsing – it took him two minutes to download the Yahoo! homepage, for instance. Unexpectedly, however, the day before the iPhone went on sale, the US AT&T EDGE network was given a massive boost, with speeds of up to 200kbps being widely reported. If these speeds are maintained, then browsing the Web on the move with an iPhone becomes fast enough to be bearable, albeit slower than 3G.

Apple has announced plans to release a 3G version of the iPhone at a later stage – possibly as soon as the European launch of the iPhone in late 2007. However, it seems unlikely that an American 3G iPhone will appear so quickly.

What about Wi-Fi?

Wi-Fi is the technology used for local-area wireless Internet connections in homes, offices, cafés and so on. Unlike current mobile phone networks, Wi-Fi networks can handle blazing-fast speeds, allowing true broadband access to any device capable of connecting to the signal.

The iPhone is Wi-Fi-friendly and will automatically connect to known wireless networks when within their range. This means that when you're at home or in the vicinity of a wireless hotspot, you'll get *much* faster Internet access than when you're out and about browsing via the EDGE network.

Wi-Fi is also known as AirPort (in Apple-speak) and IEEE 802.11x (among geeky types).

Will all websites work on an iPhone?

The iPhone features a fully-fledged Web browser – Safari – which will work with the overwhelming majority of websites. The main catch is that Flash and Java aren't currently supported. The lack of Flash means that most online animations simply won't display. That includes many banner ads (no great loss there) as well as some interactive graphics and a few entire websites.

Java is mainly used to create applications embedded within webpages – things such as online calendar tools or broadband speed tests. Though you may occasionally come across a page that requires Java, its absence isn't a huge loss.

Thankfully, Javascript, which is a very different beast to Java and totally ubiquitous on the Web, works fine.

What's Safari

Safari is the Web browser built into the iPhone. It's a streamlined version of the browser shipped on all Macs sold in the last few years. Just before the release of the iPhone in mid-2007, Apple released a version of Safari for PC users.

Safari

Does the iPhone synchronize bookmarks with my computer?

Yes. It works with Safari on Macs, and Safari or Internet Explorer on PCs. Firefox isn't currently supported.

Will the iPhone work with my email account?

For a personal email account, almost certainly. The iPhone is compatible with all standard email technologies, such as POP3 and IMAP, and even ships preset to work with AOL, Yahoo! and Gmail (known as Google Mail in some countries). If you use Outlook on a PC or Mail on a Mac, the iPhone will even sync your account details so you don't have to set anything up.

The only time you're likely to encounter problems is when setting up a work email account. This may or may not be possible, depending on the policies of your network administrators. The only way to be sure is to ask. For more on setting up and using email, see p.181.

Can I still make phone calls while on the Internet?

Yes, but only when your iPhone is connected to the Internet via a Wi-Fi network. You can't make calls and get online via EDGE simultaneously.

Can I use the iPhone to get my laptop online when out and about?

No, you can't currently use the iPhone as a wireless modem for a laptop.

iPod issues

Will the iPhone work with my iPod accessories?

Maybe. The Dock socket on the bottom of the iPhone is the same as the one on an iPod, so iPod accessories that connect via this socket should be able to connect to an  iPhone. That doesn't necessarily mean they'll work, however. At the time of writing, the success rate seems to be around 50–50.

Apple have published a list of approved accessories on their website at apple.com/iphone/accessories and have designed a "Works with iPhone" logo for products that meet their specifications.

What's the sound quality like for music?

Pretty-well the same as with an iPod. Tracks downloaded from the iTunes Store or imported from disc at the default settings sound marginally worse than CD quality. However, you're unlikely to notice any difference unless you do a side-by-side comparison through decent speakers or headphones.

Anyhow, this sound quality isn't fixed. When you import tracks from CD (or record them from vinyl) you can choose from a wide range of options, up to and including full CD quality. The only problem is that better-quality recordings take up more disk space, which means fewer tracks on your phone. The trade-off between quality and quantity is entirely for you to decide upon. For more information, see p.116.

Can I use my existing earphones or headphones?

Yes, but annoyingly you might need an adapter. Although the iPhone features a standard headphone socket (also known as

Recessed minijack socket

minijack socket or 3.5mm audio socket), it's positioned on the curved corner of the device and recessed in such a way that most regular headphone jacks won't fit.

Aside from this, if you use regular headphones or earphones, you won't be able to make use of the mic and button that form part of the supplied earbuds. These allow you to answer calls and control music playback without getting the device out of your pocket.

For details of some headphones and adapters that do work with the iPhone, turn to p.212.

Can the iPhone download music directly when I'm out and about?

No. You have to do all your downloading on your computer and then transfer that music to your iPhone.

I've never had an iPod. Isn't it a hassle to transfer all my music from CD to computer to iPhone?

It certainly takes a while to transfer a large CD collection onto your computer, but not as long as it would take to play the CDs. Depending on your computer, it can take just a few minutes to transfer the contents of a CD onto your computer's hard drive – and you can listen to the music, or work in other applications, while this is happening. Still, if you have more money than time, there are services that will take away your CDs and rip them into a well-organized collection for around $1/£1 per CD. See, for example:

PodServe podserve.co.uk (UK)
DMP3 dmp3music.com (US)
RipDigital ripdigital.com (US)

Once your music is on your PC or Mac, it only takes a matter of minutes to transfer even a large collection across to the iPhone; and subsequent transfers are even quicker, since only new or changed files are copied over.

Is downloading music and movies legal?

Yes, as long as you use a legal store such as iTunes. As for importing CDs and DVDs, the law is, surprisingly, still a tiny bit grey in many countries, but in practice no one objects to people importing their own discs for their own use.

What *could* theoretically put you on the wrong side of the law is downloading copyrighted material that you haven't acquired legitimately – and, of course, distributing copyrighted material to other people. A huge amount of music is "shared" illegally using peer-to-peer applications such as KaZaA and Limewire. With millions of people taking part, it seems impossible that everyone will get prosecuted, though there have been a few token subpoenas on either side of the Atlantic.

What's DRM?

DRM (digital rights management) is the practice of embedding special code in audio or video files to limit what the user can do with those files. For example, most of the music and video on offer at the iTunes Store includes DRM code that stops it playing back on non-Apple devices. See p.120 for more information.

02

Buying an iPhone

Which model? Where from?

For most people, buying an iPhone will involve walking into an Apple Store and simply picking whichever capacity model they can afford. But, for more cautious buyers, a few questions are going to need answering first. How much storage space do you really need? Would it be better to wait for a second-generation iPhone? These and other questions are discussed here.

Which model?

At the time of writing, there are only two iPhone models and the only difference between them is their storage capacity – 4GB or 8GB. So which to go for? That depends on the number of songs, photos, movies, podcasts and email attachments you want to be able to store at any one time.

True storage capacity

The first thing you should know is that your iPhone may offer less space than you expect. For one thing, all computer storage devices are in reality about 7 percent smaller than advertised. The reason is that hardware manufacturers use gigabyte to mean one billion bytes, whereas in computing reality it should be 2^{30}, which equals 1.0737 billion bytes. This is a bit of a scam, but everyone does it and no one wants to break the mould.

> TIP: To put the term gigabyte into perspective, 1 gigabyte (GB) is, roughly speaking, the same as a thousand megabytes (MB) or a million kilobytes (KB).

Moreover, with regard to the iPhone, nearly two hundred megabytes of the remaining 93 percent of space is used to store the phone's operating system, applications and firmware. All told, then, you can expect to lose a decent chunk of space before you even load a single song:

Advertised capacity	Real capacity	Actual free space
8GB	7.45GB	7.27GB
4GB	3.72GB	3.46GB

Checking your current data needs

If you already use iTunes to store music and video, then you can easily get an idea of how much space your existing collection takes up. On the left, click Music, Movies, Podcasts or any playlist and the bottom of the iTunes window will reveal the total disk space each one occupies.

As for photographs, the size of the images on your computer and the amount of space they occupy there bears little relation to

How big is a gig?		
		1GB =
MUSIC	at 128 kbps (normal quality)	250 typical tracks
	at 256 kbps (high quality)	125 typical tracks
	at 992 kbps (CD quality)	35 typical tracks
AUDIOBOOKS	at 32 kbps	70 hours
PHOTOS		3000 photos
VIDEO		2.5 hours

the space that the same images would take up on the iPhone. This is because when iTunes copies photos to your phone (see p.196) it resizes them for use on the iPhone's screen. As a guide, 3000 images will take up around 1GB on the phone.

Where to buy?

Unlike iPods and Macs, the iPhone is only available direct from Apple or the partner phone carrier in your country. The price will be the same.

Buying from a high-street store means you'll get the phone immediately; ordering online you can expect at least a week's wait for delivery. Another advantage of visiting a store is that you get to see the thing in the flesh and try the various features before you buy. To find your nearest Apple Store, and to check for the availability of iPhones at the various different stores, see:

Apple Stores apple.com/retail

New York City's Fifth Avenue Apple Store (on a quiet day)

Or to find the nearest branch of your carrier, see:

AT&T (US) wireless.att.com/find-a-store/iphone
O2 (UK, unconfirmed) webmap.o2.co.uk/interfaces/retail

What's in the box?

At the time of writing, the iPhone comes with a stereo headset with mic/button, a Dock, a USB charging/sync cable, a charger and a polishing cloth.

If the experience of the iPod is anything to go by, the Dock could become an optional extra in the future, if and when Apple feel pressure from competitors to lower the price.

Used iPhones

Refurbished iPhones

At the time of going to press, Apple haven't yet offered any refurbished iPhones. But if experience with iPods and Macs is anything to go by, that will change soon. Refurbished Apple products are either end-of-line models or up-to-date ones which have been returned for some reason. They come "as new" – checked, repackaged and with a full standard warranty – but they reduced in price by up to 40 percent (though usually more like 15 percent). The only problem is availability: the products are in short supply, so when you do see something listed there, you really need to make the decision to buy there and then to avoid disappointment.

You'll find the Apple Refurb Store on the bottom-right of your local Apple Store homepage.

Secondhand iPhones

Buying a secondhand iPhone is much like buying any other piece of used electronic equipment: you might find a bargain but you might land yourself with an overpriced paperweight. That said, the standard Apple warranty is transferable (in practice at least), so if you buy one that is less than a year old and comes with the documentation to prove it, you should be able to get it repaired for free if anything goes wrong inside. Obviously, that will rely on the type of damage being covered by the warranty (see p.72).

Whatever you buy, make sure you see it in action before parting with any cash, but remember that this won't tell you everything. If an iPhone has been used a lot, for example, the battery might be on its last legs and soon need replacing, which will add substantially to the cost (see p.71).

To buy or to wait?

When shopping for any piece of computer equipment, there's always the tricky question of whether to buy the current model, which may have been around for a few months, or hang on for the next version, which may be better *and* less expensive. In the case of Apple products, the situation is worse than normal, because the company is famously secretive about plans to release new or upgraded hardware.

Experience with the iPod would suggest that new iPhone models will come out every year or two. The second-generation model will probably offer 3G Internet access, more storage space (perhaps with a hard drive instead of flash chips), and perhaps even cut-down versions of Microsoft Word and Excel. Maybe it will also include the ability to make free calls via Wi-Fi.

But all this is speculation. Unless you have a friend who works in Apple HQ – and an opportunity to get them drunk – you're unlikely to hear anything from the horse's mouth until the day a new product appears. So, unless a new model came out recently, there's always the possibility that your new purchase will be out of date within a few weeks. About the best you can do is check out some sites where rumours of new models are discussed. But don't believe everything you read…

Apple Insider appleinsider.com
Mac Rumors macrumors.com
Think Secret thinksecret.com

Basics

03 Getting started

charging, syncing, typing

etting up a new
iPhone is usually a
simple process. With a
little luck, and assuming that
your computer is up to the
job (see p.18), it shouldn't
take you more than an hour
to get everything up and
running and copy across
some music, videos, photos,
contacts and calendars from
your Mac or PC. However,
you may first need to
grab the latest version of
iTunes...

Download the latest iTunes

If you've ever used an iPod, you'll already be familiar with iTunes
– Apple's application for managing music, videos and podcasts,
ripping CDs and downloading music and video. As with the iPod,
iTunes is the bridge between your computer and your iPhone.

If you use iTunes...

The iPhone requires iTunes 7.3 or higher, so even if you already use
the program, you may need to update it. New versions come out
every month or so, and it's always worth having the latest. To make
sure you have the most recent version open iTunes and, on a Mac,
choose Check
for Updates...
from the iTunes
menu and, on a
PC, look in the
Help menu.

If you don't already use iTunes...

All recent Macs have iTunes pre-installed – you'll find it in
the Applications folder. Open it up and check for updates, as
described above. If you have a PC, however, you'll need to download iTunes from Apple:

iTunes apple.com/itunes

Once you've downloaded the installer file, double-click it and follow the prompts. Either during the installation or the first time you run iTunes, you'll be presented with a few questions. Don't worry too much about these as you're just choosing options that can be changed at any time in iTunes Preferences (see p.45). But it's worth understanding what you're being asked…

▶ **Yes, use iTunes for Internet audio content** or
▶ **No, do not alter my Internet settings**
This is asking whether you'd like your computer to use iTunes (as opposed to whatever plug-ins you are currently using) as the program to handle sound and files such as MP3s when surfing the Web. iTunes can do a pretty good job of dealing with online audio, but if you'd rather stick with your existing Internet audio setup, hit No.

▶ **Yes, automatically connect to the Internet** or
▶ **No, ask me before connecting**
iTunes uses the Internet for finding CD track names or accessing the download store. If you have broadband, click Yes. If you use

43

old-school dial-up Internet, you might prefer to select No – this way you won't accidentally block your phoneline or spend extra money (if you pay per minute for access).

▶ **Do you want to search for music files on your computer and copy them to the iTunes Library?**
Unless you have music files scattered around your computer, and you'd like them automatically put in one place, select No. Otherwise you'll probably end up with random sound files in your collection. You can always import music files later (see p.125).

▶ **Do you want to go straight to the iTunes Store?**
Decline the invitation for now. For information about downloading from the Apple Store and elsewhere, see p.118.

Welcome to iTunes

Once everything's up and running you'll be presented with the iTunes window. To the left is the Source List, which contains icons for everything from playlists to connected iPhones.

iTunes essential tips

▶ **iTunes Preferences**, which is referred to throughout this book, contains a whole host of options for changing the way iTunes works. Preferences can be opened via the iTunes menu (Mac) or the Edit menu (PC). Or you could use the following shortcuts:

Apple+, (Mac)
Ctrl+, (PC)

▶ **Selecting multiple items** To select multiple tracks or other items, hold down the Apple key (Mac) or Ctrl key (PC) as you click. Alternatively, to select lots of adjacent tracks at once, click on the first and then Shift+click the last; individual songs can then be removed from this selected group by clicking them while holding down the Apple key (Mac) or the Ctrl key (PC).

▶ **Creating multiple windows** When managing and arranging your music, don't feel obliged to keep everything confined to a single iTunes panel: double-clicking a highlighted playlist or other item in the Source List will open its contents in a new floating frame.

▶ **Navigating without the mouse** Once you get the hang of it, whizzing around the iTunes window is much quicker with the keyboard than with the mouse. Use the Tab key to skip between the Source List, the search box and the main panel. To set something playing, hit the Return key.

▶ **Viewing the total playing time** Just below the main panel, iTunes displays the total amount of playing times and disk space occupied by whatever tracks or videos are visible in the main panel. Note that these are approximations; click the displayed time and it will change to an exact reading.

The iPhone at a glance

Headphone socket
Takes standard stereo minijack plugs, but many require an adapter due to the narrow recess.

SIM tray Gives access to the SIM card. To remove it, press the tiny circle with a paperclip. Non-iPhone SIMs won't work in here, but your iPhone SIM *will* work in many other phones.

Silent ringer switch Toggles between Ring and Silent mode. You choose whether vibrate is on in one or both of these modes; see p.54.

Volume buttons Affects the ringtone (when nothing's happening) or speaker/headphones (when you're on a call or playing music).

Speaker Comes on whenever you play music or video with no headphones plugged in. Also useful for calling – just press the on-screen Speaker button during a call. Anyone within a few feet can then get involved in the call.

Sleep/Wake Click
once to sleep (will still
receive calls); hold
down for three seconds
to power off (will no
longer receive calls).

Camera lens
[on the back]

Status bar Displays the time and gives you feedback about your phone via various icons. These include the following:

..ıll Phone signal level. Relates to calls rather than Internet. When abroad, you'll also see the name of the current carrier.

✈ Airplane mode on: ie phone, Wi-Fi and Bluetooth signals disabled.

🔒 Phone locked.

▶ Music or a podcast is currently playing.

🕐 Alarm set. See p.202.

🔲 Connected to EDGE network w/ Web, email and other data access . .

🛜 . . . which is replaced by this symbol when you're connected to a Wi-Fi network (see p.59). More bars means a stronger Wi-Fi signal.

✳ Bluetooth is on. See p.63.

🔋 Battery charging.

🔋 Battery fully charged.

Home button Takes you back to this
Home screen from any other screen.
Whatever you're currently doing will be
put on hold, so you can return to it later.

Mic Works well enough
from a few feet away when
using speaker phone.

Dock connector socket Takes
the iPhone sync/charge cable
– which is interchangeable with
an iPod cable. The socket is also
used for certain accessories.

Cables, Docks & charging

The iPhone comes with a charge/sync cable just like those used for the iPod. One end can attach directly to the iPhone or the supplied stand ("Dock"). The other end of the cable connects to any USB port – on a Mac or PC, on the supplied power adapter, or anywhere else.

The Dock

The Dock is a stand that makes it convenient to connect and disconnect the iPhone to computers, power sources, speakers or hi-fis. The Dock's connections can be left in place, so when you get home you simply drop your iPhone in and it's instantly hooked up, synced and charging. In addition, the Dock features a genuine line-out socket, as opposed to a headphone socket, so the sound quality is improved when connecting to hi-fi or speakers.

Note that using the Dock is entirely optional – you can also attach the cable directly to the phone. For instance, if you want to charge your iPhone at work, you may want to just take the cable with you – not the Dock.

Using iPod Docks and cables

If you have a USB cable for an iPod, this should work fine with your iPhone – and vice versa. Some iPod Docks work, too, though it depends on the model in question. If you have a Universal Dock, you can buy an inexpensive iPhone adapter for it.

One difference between the iPhone Dock and an iPod Dock is that the former offers "special audio porting" – a rather grandiloquent name for some little holes in the base of the cradle that allow you to make use of the iPhone's speaker and microphone while the device is in the Dock.

Apple's Bluetooth headset (see p.217) comes with a Dual Dock for charging the phone and headset simultaneously. These can also be purchased separately.

iPhone charging

To charge your iPhone, simply connect it to a USB port – either on a computer or a power adapter. Note, however, that if you're charging via a computer, the USB port in question will need to be "powered". The vast majority of USB sockets meet this criterion, but some, especially those on keyboards and other peripherals, may not work. Also note that your iPhone usually won't charge from a Mac or PC in sleep or standby mode.

When the iPhone is charging the battery icon at the top-right of the screen will display a lightning slash. When it's fully charged this will change to a plug. When your phone is plugged in and not in use, you'll also see a large battery icon across its centre, which shows how charged it is at present.

Like many similar devices, iPhones use a combination of "fast" and "trickle" charging. This means that it should take around two hours to achieve an 80 percent charge, and another two hours to get to 100 percent. A new, fully charged iPhone should provide the following performance. However, as the battery ages, expect these times to reduce.

8 hours of talk time

or **6 hours of Web and email**

or **250 hours on standby**

or **7 hours of Video playback**

or **24 hours of music playback**

If your iPhone's power becomes so low that the device can't function, you may well find that plugging in to start charging will not revive it straight away. Don't worry – it should come back to life after ten minutes or so.

If you're in a hurry to charge, don't use or sync the iPhone while it's charging – this will slow the charge process. You can cancel the sync with the slider on the iPhone screen – or by "ejecting" the phone in iTunes (see overleaf).

For tips on maximizing your battery life see p.69.

Activating

Once you have the latest version of iTunes installed, and your iPhone is connected to your computer, you're ready to activate the phone and copy across any data and media from your computer. This shouldn't take long, though there could be delays if your carrier is overloaded with activation requests (as happened for a few days after the launch in the US).

Within iTunes, follow the prompts to register with Apple's partner carrier in your country, transfer your old number and choose a tariff. As part of the process you'll need to enter your iTunes account details (Apple ID or .Mac details will also work). If you don't have an account, you'll need to set one up – even if you have no intention of buying any music or video via iTunes.

Note that both your activation fee (where applicable) and monthly service-plan payments are billed direct to your carrier – *not* your iTunes account.

Disconnecting an iPhone

Unlike an iPod, an iPhone doesn't batten down its hatches when connected to your computer. All its functions remain available – you can even make calls. Likewise, whereas an iPod sometimes needs to be properly "ejected" before it can be disconnected, the iPhone can be disconnected at any time, even halfway through a sync. Despite this, iTunes still offers an eject button ⏏ next to the iPhone's icon. This allows you to remove the iPhone from iTunes but leave it charging.

Synchronizing

Once the activation process is complete, you'll find yourself presented with the various tabs that control how the iPhone is synchronized with your computer. These include the following, each of which is covered in more detail elsewhere in this book.

▶ **Info** Lets you synchronise contacts (see p.77), mail accounts (see p.182), calendars (see p.200) and bookmarks (see p.174) from your computer. Once set up, changes or additions made on the computer will be reflected on your phone, and vice versa.

▶ **Music, podcasts & video** Lets you copy across some or all of your iTunes content over to the iPhone. You can't add audio or video to the iPhone directly, but you can create playlists and track ratings which are moved back to iTunes when you next connect.

> TIP: If you receive a call while iTunes is performing a sync, the sync will be cancelled to allow you to answer the call. So remember to reconnect the phone after you've hung up, to allow the sync to finish.

▶ **Photos** iTunes moves photos from your selected application or folder (see p.196) and gives you the option, each time you connect, to import photos taken with the iPhone's camera onto your computer.

Forcing a sync

When you choose from any of the above options, click Apply Now to start syncing straight away. You can also initiate a sync at any time by right-clicking the icon for your iPhone (Ctrl-click on a Mac) and choosing Sync from the dropdown menu.

Seeing what's on your iPhone

At any time while connected, you can click the triangle to the left of your iPhone's iTunes icon to see the music, video and podcasts that it's currently storing.

Syncing with multiple computers

When you connect your iPhone to a different computer, it will appear in iTunes (7.3 or higher required) with all the sync options unchecked. You can then skip through the various tabs and choose to overwrite some or all of the current content…

▶ **Music, video & podcasts** Adding music, video or podcasts from a second computer will erase all of the existing media from the phone, since an iPhone can only be synced with one iTunes Library at a time. You'll also lose any on-the-go playlists and track ratings entered since your last sync. Next time you connect at home, you can reload your own media, but you won't be able to copy the new material back onto your computer.

▶ **Photos** can be synced from a new machine without affecting music, video or any other content. However, to leave everything other than photos intact, you need to hit Cancel when iTunes offers to synchronize the "Account Information" from the new machine.

▶ **Info** When you add contacts, calendars, email accounts or bookmarks from a second computer, you have two choices – either merging the new data and existing data, or simply overwriting the existing data. iTunes will ask you which way you want to play it when you check the box for a category and click Apply. However, you can bypass this by scrolling down to the bottom of the Info panel and checking the relevant overwrite boxes.

Basic set-up options

Once your iPhone is stocked up with all your media and data, you're ready to make it your own…

Ringtones and alerts

Tap Settings > Sounds > Ringtones to play through the various options. Within the Sounds page you can also toggle various alert sounds on and off, and choose a volume level for your chosen ringtone (this does the same as using the volume buttons on the side of the phone).

Ring, vibrate and silent

The iPhone offers two modes – Ring and Silent – which you can switch between using the switch on the left-hand side of the phone. You can choose to have the phone vibrate in one or both of these modes. Click settings, then Sounds to make your selection.

Wallpaper

Tap Settings > Wallpaper to choose the photo that appears on your screen when you wake the iPhone from sleep mode. You can drag and crop the photo before setting it. (When doing so, if

> TIP: You will probably want to change the unimaginative name that iTunes gives your iPhone during activation. To do this, tap on the name next to the iPhone icon in iTunes and retype whatever you want.

you set the top and bottom edges of a horozontal photo to align with the edges of the semi-transparent zones, the pic will appear framed by, rather than behind, the strips when the phone awakes from sleep.)

Auto-Lock

Within Settings > General, you can set the number of minutes of inactivity before your iPhone goes to sleep and locks its screen. In order to maximize battery life, leave it set to 1 minute unless you find this setting annoying.

Privacy

If you want to protect the private data on your phone – and make

sure no one ever uses it to make calls without your permission – apply a passcode. Tap Settings > General > Passcode Lock, and choose a 4-digit number. With this feature turned on, the phone can't be unlocked after waking from sleep without first entering the number. If you forget the code, connect your phone to your computer and restore it (see p.67). If a thief tries this, they'll get the phone working, but by that stage all your private data will no longer be on the phone.

> TIP: Another less serious privacy risk is that, when you receive an SMS, the message will pop up on the screen even if the phone is locked. If you'd rather this didn't happen, turn off SMS Preview within the Passcode Lock page.

Typing tips

The iPhone's touch-screen keyboard isn't to everyone's taste, but if you can get used to it, the iPhone allows for typing far faster than almost any of its competitors. Following are some tips to get you started. The best place to practice is in the Notes application (see p.205).

Basic techniques

▶ **Pop-up keys** The iPhone enters a letter or symbol when you *release* your finger, not when you touch the screen. So if you're struggling to type accurately (or you're entering a password and can't see what you're typing) try tapping and holding the letter. If the wrong letter pops up, slide to the correct one and then release.

▶ **Numbers and punctuation** To reveal these keys, tap .?123.

▶ **Symbols** To reveal these keys, tap .?123 followed by #+=.

▶ **Making edits** You can tap anywhere in your text to jump to that point. For more accuracy, tap, hold and then slide around to see a magnifying glass containing a cursor.

Auto-correct and prediction

It may be hard to hit every key accurately on the iPhone, but usually that doesn't matter much, thanks to the device's ingenious word-prediction software. Even if you hit only half the right letters, the phone will usually work out what you meant by looking at the keys adjacent to the ones you tapped and comparing each permutation of letters to those in its dictionary or words and phrases.

Accepting and rejecting suggestions
When the iPhone suggests a word or name it will appear in a little bubble under the word you're typing. To accept the suggestion, just keep typing as normal – hit space, return or a punctuation mark. To reject it, finish typing the word and then tap the suggestion before continuing.

Dictionary
The iPhone has a much bigger and more relevant dictionary than most mobile phones – including, for example, many names and swear words. In addition, it learns all names stored in your contacts and any word that you've typed twice, in both cases rejecting the suggested correction. Unfortunately, it's not currently possible to edit the dictionary, but you can blank it and start again. Tap Settings > General > Reset > Reset Keyboard Dictionary.

▶ **Auto-capitalization** In addition to correcting letters, the iPhone will add puncuation (changing "Im" to "I'm", for example) and capitalize the first letter of words at the start of sentences. If you prefer to stick with lowercase, turn off Auto-capitalization within Settings > General > Keyboard.

Speed-typing tips

▶ **One-touch punctuation** Tap .?123 and then slide to the relevant key without taking your finger off the screen. Much more convenient than tapping twice.

▶ **One-touch caps** The same trick works with capital letters: tap shift and slide to a letter.

▶ **Caps Lock** If you like to TYPE IN CAPS, turn on the Caps Lock feature under Settings > General > Keyboard. Once that's done, you can double-tap Shift to toggle Caps Lock on and off.

▶ **Thumbs and fingers** Apple recommend that you start off using just your index finger and progress to two thumbs. However, you could also try multiple fingers on one hand. This can be even faster, since thumbs tend to bump into each other when aiming at keys near the middle of the keyboard, though it does take a little getting used to.

▶ **One touch at a time** If typing with two thumbs or multiple fingers, only let one finger touch the screen at a time. If the first finger is still on the screen, the second tap won't be recognized.

▶ **Web keyboard** In Safari, but not other applications, you can rotate the iPhone to get a bigger version of the keyboard.

To measure your iPhone typing skills in terms of words per minute, tap Safari and visit: iphonetypingtest.com. Another good iPhone typing trainer can be found at: voxifera.com/itypex

Connecting

Wi-Fi, Bluetooth and other airwaves

The first-generation iPhone can handle four kinds of wireless signal: GSM, for mobile phone calls; EDGE, for mobile Internet access; Wi-Fi, for Internet access in homes, offices and public hotspots; and Bluetooth, for connecting to compatible headsets and carphone systems. This chapter takes a quick look at each.

Airplane mode

Airplane mode, quickly accessible at the top of the Settings menu, lets you temporarily disable GSM, EDGE, Wi-Fi and Bluetooth, enabling you to use non-wireless features such as iPod during a flight or in any other circumstances where mobile phone use is not permitted. (Whether phones actually cause any risk on aircraft is disputed, but that's another story.) Airport mode can also be useful if you want to make sure you don't incur roaming charges when overseas by inadvertently checking your mail and so on.

Using Wi-Fi

Connecting to networks

To connect to a Wi-Fi network, tap Settings > Wi-Fi and choose a network from the list. If it's a secure wireless network (as indicated by the padlock icon), the iPhone will invite you to enter the relevant password.

Though this procedure doesn't take long, it's best to have the iPhone point you in the direction of Wi-Fi networks automatically. This way, whenever you open an Internet-based tool such as Maps or Mail, and there are no known networks in range, the iPhone will automatically present you with a list of all the networks it can find. You can turn this feature on and off via Settings > Wi-Fi > Ask to Join Networks.

If the network you want to connect to isn't in the list, you could be out of range, or it could be that it's a "hidden" network, in which case tap Wi-Fi > Other and enter its name, password and password type.

> **TIP:** If you want to maximize battery life, get into the habit of turning Wi-Fi off when you're not using it. It only takes a couple of seconds to turn it back on when you next need it.

Forgetting networks

Once you've connected to a Wi-Fi network, your iPhone will remember it as a trusted network and connect to it automatically

Finding public hotspots

Many cafés, hotels, airports and other public places offer free wireless Internet access, though often you'll have to pay for the privilege of using them – particularly in establishments which are part of big chains (Starbucks and the like). You either pay the person running the system (over the counter in a café, for instance) or connect and sign up on-screen. If you use such services a lot, you may save time and money by signing up with a service such as Boingo, T-Mobile or Wayport, which allow you to connect at thousands of hotspots for a monthly fee.

Boingo boingo.com
T-Mobile t-mobile.com/hotspot
Wayport wayport.com

The ideal, of course, is to stick to free hotspots. There are various online directories that will help you locate them, though none is comprehensive:

Hotspot Locations hotspot-locations.com
WiFinder wifinder.com
Wi-Fi Free Spot wififreespot.com
ZONE Finder wi-fi.jiwire.com

whenever you're in range. This is useful, though can be annoying – if, for example, it keeps connecting to a network you once chose accidentally, or one which lets you connect but doesn't provide Web access. In these cases, click on the ⓘ icon next to the relevant network name and tap Forget This Network. This won't stop you connecting to it manually in the future.

When it won't connect…

If your iPhone refuses to connect to a Wi-Fi network, try again, in case you mistyped the password or tapped the wrong network name. If you still have no luck, try the following:

▶ **Try WEP Hex** If there's a ⓘ icon in the password box, tap it, choose WEP Hex and try again.

▶ **Check the settings** Some networks, especially in offices, require you to manually enter information such as an IP address. Ask your network administrator for the details and plug them in by clicking ◉ next to the relevant network name.

▶ **Add your MAC address** Some routers in homes and offices (but not in public hotspots) will only allow access to a list of pre-approved devices. If this is the case, you'll need to enter the phone's MAC address – which you'll find within Settings > General > About > Wi-Fi Address – to your router's list. This usually means entering the router's setup screen and looking for something titled MAC Filtering or Access List.

▶ **Reboot the router** If you're at home, try rebooting your wireless router by turning it off or unplugging it for a few seconds. Turn off the Wi-Fi on the phone (Settings > Wi-Fi) until the router has rebooted.

▶ **Tweak your router settings** If the above doesn't work, try temporarily turning off your router's wireless password to see whether that fixes the problem. If it does, try choosing a different type of password (WEP rather than WPA, for example). If that doesn't help, you could try updating the firmware (internal software) of the router, in case the current version isn't compatible with the iPhone's hardware. Check the manufacturer's website to see if a firmware update is available.

Test your speed

To test the speed and latency (time lag) of your current EDGE or Wi-Fi signal, tap Safari and visit the following site.

iPhone Speed Test i.dslr.net/tinyspeedtest.html

GSM & EDGE

In your home country, the iPhone should automatically connect to your carrier's GSM and EDGE networks whenever you're in range – that is, unless you've switched on Airport Mode. As dicussed on p.25, EDGE is much slower than proper broadband, so it will automatically give way to Wi-Fi whenever possible.

Connecting abroad

When you're overseas, Wi-Fi will work normally, but in order to use GSM or EDGE you may have to activate international roaming. (This is certainly true for American iPhone users, though it seems unlikely the same will apply when the phone is released in Europe.) Once that's done, you can use any overseas carrier that has a roaming agreement with your home carrier.

You'll probably find that your phone selects foreign carriers automatically. If you prefer, however, it's possible to specify a preference. Simply tap Settings > Carrier and pick from the list.

For more on international roaming, including sample AT&T rates, see p.23.

Bluetooth

Bluetooth allows computers, phones, printers and other devices to communicate at high speeds over short distances. As already discussed, however, Apple have disabled all Bluetooth activity on the iPhone except connecting to mono headsets and certain carphone systems. Other devices may recognize the presence of an iPhone, but they can't communicate with it in any useful way.

You can turn Bluetooth on and off by tapping Settings > General > Bluetooth. If you're not using it, leave it switched off to help maximize battery life.

VPN & remote access

VPN access

If your office network uses a VPN (Virtual Private Network) to allow access to file servers, email, webpages or whatever, you'll probably find that your iPhone can connect to it. The phone supports most VPN systems (specifically, those which use L2TP or PPTP protocols), so ask your administrator for details and enter them under Settings > General > Network > VPN.

Remote access

Since the iPhone can connect to the Internet, there's no reason it can't directly access a computer that's also online – a Mac or PC in your home or office, say. Once set up, you could, for example, stream music and video from your iTunes collection or browse your files. All you need is the correct software and security settings on the computer in question.

Within weeks of the iPhone's launch, special remote-management software was created for both Macs and PCs. At the time of writing, both systems are aimed at programmers rather than the average user. But consumer-focused versions will doubtless emerge soon, so keep an eye out, starting here:

iPhone Remote (Mac) code.google.com/p/telekinesis
WebVNC Remote Desktop (PC) cre.ations.net/creator/natetrue

Maintenance

Troubleshooting and battery tips

The iPhone is a tiny computer and, just like its full-sized cousins, it will occasionally crash or become unresponsive. Far less common, and much more serious, is hardware failure, which will require you to send the phone away for servicing. This chapter gives advice for both situations, along with tips for maximizing battery life.

Crashes and software problems

You should expect, every now and again, your iPhone to crash or generally behave in strange ways. This will more often than not be a problem with a specific application, and the iPhone will simply throw you out of the app and take you back to the Home screen. From there, simply tap your way back to where you were and start again. If the screen completely freezes, however, try force-quitting the current application by holding down the Home button for about five or six seconds. If the problem persists, try the following steps, in this order...

▶ **Reboot** As with any other computer, turning an iPhone off and back on often solves software problems. To turn the phone off, press and hold the Sleep/Wake button for a couple of seconds and then slide the red switch to confirm. Count to five, and then press and hold the Sleep/Wake button again to reboot.

▶ **Reset** If that doesn't do the trick, or you can't get your phone to turn off, try resetting your phone. This won't harm any music or data on the device. Press and hold the Sleep/Wake button and the Home button at the same time for around ten seconds. The phone may first display the regular shutdown screen and red confirm switch; ignore it, and keep holding the buttons, only letting go when the Apple logo appears.

▶ **Reset All Settings** Still no joy? Resetting your iPhone's preferences may help. All your current settings will be lost, but no data or media is deleted. Tap Settings > General > Reset > Reset All Settings.

▶ **Erase all content** If that doesn't work, you could try deleting all the media and data, too, by tapping Settings > General > Reset > Erase All Content and Settings. Then connect the iPhone to your computer and restore your previously backed-up settings (see box on p.68) and copy all your media back onto the phone.

iPhone firmware

Just as it's always a good idea to run the latest version of iTunes on your Mac or PC, it's also worth running the latest version of the iPhone's internal software – also known as firmware. The phone's firmware will be automatically updated from time to time when your computer is online and connected to the phone. This doesn't affect your settings, media or data, but it fixes bugs and will make the iPhone run more smoothly.

> TIP: If you are having problems with Wi-Fi connections,
> try tapping the Reset Network Settings button on the
> Reset screen described above.

▶ **Restore** This will restore the iPhone's software either to the original factory settings or to the settings recorded in the most recent automatic backup (see box overleaf). In both cases all data, settings and media are deleted from the phone. Connect the iPhone to your computer and, within the Summary tab of the phone's options pane, click Restore and follow the prompts.

▶ **Firmware update** The iPhone's internal software should update itself automatically (see box). But you can check for new versions at any time by opening iTunes, connecting your phone and, on the summary screen, clicking "Check for Update". If a new version is available, install it.

Backing up

iTunes automatically creates a backup of key data on your iPhone whenever you connect to your computer. This can be useful if, for example, you lose your phone and have to replace it with a new one.

The backup includes mail settings, SMS messages, notes, call history and Favorites list, sound settings and other preferences. It doesn't include music, video and picture files (since these are already stored in your iTunes Library), photos (which should also be safely residing on your computer) or contacts (which, hopefully, you will have copied across to Address Book or Outlook).

To view, and if necessary delete, an automatic iPhone backup, open iTunes Preferences and click iPhone in the strip along the top. To restore to a backup, simply connect an iPhone and click Restore in the iPhone Summary pane within iTunes.

Of course, the backup – and indeed all your media files – is only as safe as your Mac or PC. Computers can die, get destroyed or be stolen, so get into the habit of backing up to either an external hard drive or write-able DVDs. For more on this subject, see *The Rough Guide to Macs & OS X*.

The iPhone battery

There has been a fair amount of controversy, and no shortage of misinformation, about the iPhone's non-user-replaceable battery (see p.20). Like all lithium-ion batteries, the one inside the iPhone lasts for a certain amount of time before starting to lose its ability to hold a full charge. According to Apple, this reduction in capacity will happen after around 400 "charge cycles".

Despite various newspaper reports to the contrary, a charge cycle counts as one full running down and recharging of the battery. So if you use, say, 20 percent of the battery each day and then top it back up to full, the total effect will be one charge cycle every five days; in this situation the battery would, theoretically, only start to lose its ability to hold a full charge after quite a few years: 5 days x 400 charge cycles = 2000 days.

If, on the other hand, you drain your battery twice a day by watching DVDs while commuting to and from work, you might see your battery deteriorate after just nine months or so. In this case, you'd get it replaced for free, as the iPhone would still be within warranty.

If the battery won't charge

If your iPhone won't charge up via your computer, it could be that the USB port you're connected to doesn't supply enough power or that your Mac or PC is going into standby mode during the charge. To make sure the phone is OK, try charging via the supplied power adapter. If this doesn't work either, it could be the cable; if you have an iPod cable lying around, try that instead, or borrow one from a friend. If you still can't get it to charge, send the phone for servicing (see p.71).

Tips for maximizing battery life

Following are various techniques for minimizing the demands on your iPhone battery. Each one will help ensure that each charge last for as long as possible *and* that your battery's overall lifespan is maximized.

▶ **Keep it cool** Avoid leaving your iPhone in direct sunlight or anywhere hot. Apple state that the device works best at 0–35°C (32–95°F), but as a general rule, try to keep it at room temperature.

▶ **Keep it updated** One of the things that firmware updates can help with is battery efficiency. So be sure to accept any iPhone software updates on offer through iTunes.

▶ **Drain it** As with all lithium-ion batteries, it's a good idea to run your iPhone completely flat at least once a month and then fully charge it again.

▶ **Dim it** Screen brightness makes a big difference to battery life, so if you think you could live with less of it, turn down the slider within Settings > Brightness. Experiment with and without the Auto-Brightness option, which adjusts screen brightness according to ambient light levels.

▶ **Lock it** Press the Sleep/Wake button when you've finished a call to avoid wasting energy by accidentally tapping the screen in your pocket before the phone locks itself.

▶ **Turn off Wi-Fi & Bluetooth** These are both power-hungry features which are easily turned off when not in use. Use the switches under Settings > Wi-Fi and Settings > General > Bluetooth.

▶ **Junk the EQ** Set your iPhone to use Flat EQ settings. This will knock out imported iTunes EQ settings, which can increase battery demands.

▶ **Stay lo-fi** High-bitrate music formats such as Apple Lossless may improve the sound quality (see p.116), but they also increase the power required for playback.

When the battery dies

When your battery no longer holds enough charge to fulfil its function, you'll need to replace it. The official solution is to send the phone to Apple, who, if your phone is no longer within

The iPhone battery, pictured as part of iFixit's guide to disassembling the device. For the full guide, see: ifixit.com/Guide/iPhone

its warranty period, will charge you $76, inclusive of shipping (European prices have yet to be confirmed). You'll get the phone back after three working days, but if you can't wait that long, you could hire a replacement for $29.

The unofficial solution is to try and find a less expensive battery from a third-party service, along with a fitting service or DIY instructions. At the time of writing, this isn't an option, but it seems likely that the companies which already offer iPod battery replacements will soon expand their range. These include:

iPod Battery ipodbattery.com
iPod Juice ipodjuice.com

iPhone repairs

If the advice in this chapter hasn't worked, try going online and searching for help in the sites and forums listed on p.232. If that doesn't clear things up, it could be that you'll need to have your phone repaired by Apple. To do this, you could take it to an Apple retail store (see p.35), though be warned that in some cases you may have to make an appointment.

Alternatively, visit the following website and fill out a service request form. Apple will send you an addressed box in which you can return your phone to them. It will arrive back by post.

Apple Service Depot apple.com/support/service/depot

Either way, you're advised to remove your SIM card before sending it off (see p.46) and you can choose to hire a replacement iPhone for the period of repair ($29 in the US, price not yet confirmed elsewhere). But make sure you return it on time, or you'll be charged a $50 fee or the full price of the phone depending on the length of the delay.

Warranty, AppleCare and insurance

The iPhone comes with a one-year warranty that covers everything you'd expect (hardware failure and so on) and nothing that you wouldn't (accidents, loss, theft and unauthorized service). The only departure form the norm is that while most Apple mobile products come with a warranty that enables you to take the faulty device to any Apple dealer around the world, the iPhone warranty currently only covers the country in which you purchased it.

In addition, you can choose to extend your warranty by a further two years through the AppleCare scheme. The price isn't confirmed at the time of writing, though is expected to be around $60. Assuming AppleCare will include iPhone battery cover, that isn't a bad deal for anyone who expects to regularly use their phone for power-hungry activities such as video watching.

AppleCare apple.com/support/products

As for insurance against accidental damage and theft, AT&T surprised many commentators by not offering an iPhone insurance option at the time of launch. It remains to be seen whether this will also be true for carriers in the UK and other countries. Either way, you could investigate what options are available via your home-contents scheme. Many insurers offer away-from-home coverage for high-value items – though it can be expensive.

Diagnostic codes

Many phones respond to diagnostic codes – special numbers that, when dialled, reveal information about your account, network or handset on the screen. Assembled in part from a post at The Unofficial Apple Weblog (tuaw.com, essential reading for all Mac, iPod and iPhone users), the following list includes many such codes for the iPhone. Some are specific to AT&T or the iPhone, while others will work on any phone.

Note that these are American codes. European iPhone users may find that only a few of them work on their handsets.

▶ *#06#
Displays the IMEI – the handset's unique identification code.

▶ *225# Call
Displays current monthly balance.

▶ *646# Call
Displays remaining monthly minutes.

▶ *777# Call
Displays account balance for a prepaid iPhone.

▶ *#61# Call
Displays the total numbers of calls forwarded to voicemail when the phone was unanswered.

▶ *#62# Call
Displays the total numbers of calls forwarded to voicemail when the phone had no service.

▶ *#67# Call
Displays the total numbers of calls forwarded to voicemail when the phone was engaged.

▶ *#21# Call
Displays various Call Forwarding settings.

▶ *#30# Call
Displays whether or not your phone is set to display the numbers of incoming callers.

▶ *#43# Call
Displays whether call waiting is enabled.

▶ *#33# Call
Displays whether call barring is enabled for outgoing calls.

▶ *3001#12345#* Call
Activates Field Test mode, which reveals loads of hidden iPhone and network settings and data. Don't mess with these unless you know exactly what you're doing.

Phone

06 Contacts

Importing, syncing & managing

J ust like every other mobile phone, the iPhone allows you to store a list of names and phone numbers. Unlike some other phones, it also lets you store all kinds of other information for a contact – from their email and fax to home address, birthday and job title.

You can fill in as much or as little as you like. Even better, the iPhone makes it easy to synchronize your contacts info with the address book on your computer. This is not only convenient, but means that your precious names and numbers can be safely backed up.

If you've been living on the moon for the last decade, you might wish to start your contacts list from scratch, in which case turn to p.86. Probably, however, you'll want to import the contacts from your old phone or computer…

Importing contacts from a phone

At the time of writing, the iPhone can't communicate with other mobile phones via Bluetooth, it won't read most SIM cards, and it can't receive contact cards via email. So your best bet for importing contacts from an old phone is to copy them across from the old phone to your computer, into one of the address book applications that the iPhone can communicate with. This way you'll also be able to tidy up and consolidate your contacts info on your computer before moving everything over to the iPhone.

Of course, if you only have a few numbers on your old phone, or the following techniques seem like too much hassle, you could always manually enter your numbers into your computer (see p.82) or iPhone (see p.87).

Moving contacts from an old phone to a Mac

With Bluetooth

First you need to pair your phone and Mac. To do this, make sure the phone is "discoverable", an option usually found under Connectivity or Bluetooth. Next, on your Mac, click…

 > System Preferences > Bluetooth > Devices > Set Up New Device

… and follow the prompts. Once that's all done, open iSync from your Mac's Applications folder and choose Add Device from the Devices menu. With any luck, your phone will be recognized and appear on the toolbar. Choose what you want to copy across

> TIP: Most Macs and many PCs shipped in the last few years have Bluetooth built in; for those which don't, this feature can also be added with an inexpensive USB adapter. **Bluetooth**

Apple's iSync application, included on all recent Macs, makes it simple to import numbers from mobile phones

(contacts, calendars or both), hit the Sync Devices button and the data should be imported from the phone into your Mac's Address Book, ready for transfer to your iPhone. Turn to p.82 for more on using Address Book.

Don't have Bluetooth?

If your phone or Mac lack Bluetooth, you could buy the appropriate cable to connect your phone directly to your Mac (ask in any phone store) and use iSync as described above.

Alternatively, you could try a SIM reader to extract vCard or text files from the phone. These files can then be imported into the address book on your computer, ready to be synced with the iPhone.

SIM readers

A SIM reader is an inexpensive device that will feed numbers stored on a mobile phone SIM card into a Mac or PC via a USB socket.

Before using a SIM reader, you'll need to make sure that the numbers on the phone are stored on the SIM rather than in the phone's memory. Consult the manual to find out how this is done (you can probably download the manual if you no longer have it). Then remove the SIM, insert it into the reader and connect it to your computer. You'll probably be left with vCard or text files, which should be easy to import into Address Book, Outlook or Outlook Express (look for the Import option in the File menu).

If you're unlucky, and you can't get the files to import, try opening them with Text Edit (Mac) or Notepad (PC). You should then at least be able to see the data from your phone and, if needs be, copy and paste it into new contact cards.

Moving contacts from an old phone to a PC

The iPhone can pull contacts from either Outlook Express (ie the Windows XP Address Book) or Outlook on a PC. Unfortunately, getting numbers from your phone into one of these applications can be tricky, because Windows doesn't ship with a simple tool for moving data from phone to PC.

If your phone came with a CD, it may contain software that will let you export the numbers to your phone as vCards or text files, either via Bluetooth or a cable. In most cases, these files can be dropped into Outlook or the Windows XP Address Book (choose Import in the File menu).

Alternatively, you could buy a downloadable number-transfer tool such as the following. These cost $20–40 but will help you copy across photos and movies, as well as contact info:

DataPilot datapilot.com
Mobile Master mobile-master.com
WinFonie Mobile 2 bertels-hirsch.de/en/winfonie_mobile_2

Finally, you could try a SIM reader (see box) or ask for help in a phone store. For a small fee, some stores will pull the numbers off your old phone and provide them on a CD or flash drive, ready to be imported into your contact application of choice. Similar services are available online from sites such as:

CelluarDr cellulardr.com (US only)

From old phone to the Yahoo! Address Book

iTunes can sync contact info between your Yahoo! Mail address book and your iPhone. So one final option for getting the numbers off your old phone is to upload them directly to Yahoo!. If you currently have a smart phone or handheld that runs Palm OS, this can be done by using Yahoo!'s Intellisync feature – look for the "Sync" button on your Yahoo! Mail homepage to see how it can be set up. Regular mobile phone users can take a look at what's on offer from the Yahoo! Go service (mobile.yahoo.com/go), though not all handsets are compatible.

Editing contacts on a computer

However you get the numbers from your old phone to your computer, it's likely that the result will need some editing – duplicates culled, email addresses and other information added, and so on. All this can be done on the iPhone (as we'll see), but it's easier on a computer.

It's beyond the scope of this book to walk you through contact management in Address Book, Outlook and Outlook Express, but here are some general pointers:

▶ **Default formats** Look within your Preferences or Options to check that the default address and phone number format is correct for the country where you live.

▶ **Groups** You can add contacts in your address book to "groups" or "distribution lists". You might have all your work colleagues in one group, say, and all your friends and family in another. When you sync your iPhone you can choose to copy across either all contacts or just selected groups.

▶ **Duplicate entries** After you import the contacts from an old phone, you may well end up with duplicated entries. The Apple Address Book boasts a "Merge Contact" feature that can resolve the problem: click Apple+1 to view your contacts as Cards and Columns; next, search for the duplicated contact's name, select the two entries when holding down the Apple key and

> TIP: On a Mac, you can choose to have all the websites
> associated with your contacts in Address Book added to
> your bookmarks in Safari. In Safari Preferences, under
> the Bookmarks tab, check the various "Include Address Book"
> boxes.

choose Merge Selected Cards from the Cards menu. Outlook, meanwhile, will automatically alert you when duplicate entries appear and ask you how you want to resolve the conflict. To check whether this feature is enabled, open Options from the Tools menu.

▶ **Pictures** Though time consuming and not particularly useful, adding images to contacts can be a fun way to personalize your Address Book on your computer and, in turn, your iPhone. It can be especially useful if you are the kind of person who finds it hard to put names to faces.

Though you could, of course, take snaps out and about with the iPhone itself and associate those images with your contacts there and then (see p.195), pictures can also be added to your computer's address book. On a Mac, simply drag a photo onto an entry. Of course, you don't even have to use mug shots: if, like both Apple and Microsoft, you think an individual might be best represented by, say, a tennis ball or a butterfly, then so be it.

Syncing contacts with the iPhone

Open iTunes, connect your iPhone and select its icon in the Source panel. You'll find the Contacts options under the "Info" tab. Check the relevant sync option and choose whether you want to import all contacts or just particular groups. Once that's done, each time you connect your iPhone, any new contact information added on the computer will be copied across to the phone, and vice versa.

Syncing contacts with Entourage

Apple describe Entourage – the Mac version of Outlook – as being compatible with the iPhone in terms of syncing contacts and calendars. But this isn't possible directly. In order to enable syncing between the iPhone and Entourage, you first have to enable syncing between Entourage and the Apple Address Book. To do this, open Entourage and choose Preferences from the Entourage menu. Under Sync Services, check Contacts and Events. If you can't find these options, you may need to update your software. Click Check for Updates in the Entourage Help menu.

In addition, if you use Yahoo! Mail you may want to opt to import the email addresses and other contact information stored in your Yahoo! address book. If you select Yahoo! *and* another contacts source, you'll find that these two sources become synchronized with each other, so you'll end up with the same amalgamated contacts database on your phone, your Yahoo! account and your computer.

Plaxo: syncing contacts with Gmail, AOL, etc

As we've seen, iTunes can sync with contacts in Address Book, Outlook and Outlook Express, and Yahoo! Mail. If you have contact info in Gmail, AOL, Hotmail or Thunderbird, you'll be interested in Plaxo, a free online contact and calendar management tool co-created by one of the names behind Napster, Sean Parker. Plaxo can merge and update address books from all the services just mentioned, in addition to those which iTunes can handle. So you could use it to get all your contacts onto your PC or Mac, and from there onto your iPhone.

Contacts on the iPhone

You'll find the iPhone's main Contacts list as one of the five buttons when you tap Phone. To browse the list, either flick up or down with your finger, or drag your finger over the alphabetic list on the right to quickly navigate to a specific letter – useful if you have an extensive list of contacts. Thankfully, this combination of

Flick up and down to hone in on a specific contact

Tap once to stop a moving list in its place

Drag up and down the alphabet to speed to a specific letter

> TIP: By default the iPhone alphabetizes your contacts by
> surname. You can change this by clicking Settings on the
> main screen and looking under Phone.

flicking and dragging works very well, since there's no keyboard-based way of jumping to or searching for a contact.

When you find the contact you want, tap once to view all their details, and then tap a phone number to start a call or an email address to launch a new mail message.

Adding contacts

There are various ways to add new contacts on the iPhone.

▶ **In Contacts** When viewing your contacts list, click the + at the top right.

▶ **From the keypad** You can enter a number via the keypad (found under Phone) and then tap the head-and-shoulders graphic to the left of the call button. From there you can choose to create a new contact or add the number to an existing contact.

▶ **From the recent calls list** When viewing recent calls (under Phone), you can tap the ⊙ icon next to an unrecognized number and choose to create a new contact or add to an exising contact.

Favorites

The Favorites list, found from the Phone screen, provides quick access to your most frequently dialled numbers. Instead of full contacts, it stores a specific number for each name. This way you can dial with just a couple of clicks – much quicker than browsing through a long contacts list, selecting a person and then picking from their home, work and mobile numbers.

▶ **To add Favorites**, browse your contacts and click the relevant names, in each case choosing Add to Favorites and picking a number. Alternatively, from Favorites, hit the + button to browse for names.

▶ **To change the order** of your Favorites, tap the Edit button and drag contacts by their right-hand edge (pictured).

▶ **To remove a Favorite** click Edit, tap the red ● icon next to the relevant name, and then hit Remove.

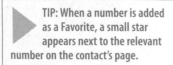

> TIP: When a number is added as a Favorite, a small star appears next to the relevant number on the contact's page.

Editing contacts

To edit a contact – change their
name or number, assign a specific
ringtone, add an email address, or
whatever – simply click the relevant
name in the main contacts list and
hit Edit. Then…

▶ Use the Add options, signified by
a green ⊕, to add a new number,
address or other attribute.

▶ If you can't see the relevant
attribute, click Add Field. You'll
then be offered everything from
birthday to a space for notes. This
info may then be useful back on
your computer. For instance, if you
add birthdays, these can sync with
your calendar application, which you
could set up to automatically send
you a reminder email a day or two
before each friend or relative's birthday.

▶ To delete an item, tap its red ⊖ icon. To delete the contact from
your Contacts list entirely, scroll down to the bottom of the entry
and tap the "Delete Contact" button.

> ▶ TIP: Syncing with Yahoo! won't delete any contact entry
> in the Yahoo! Address Book that contains an ID for Yahoo!
> Messenger, even if you delete that contact on the iPhone
> or your computer. To delete such a contact, log in to your Yahoo!
> account and remove it directly.

▶ To assign a picture to a contact, click Add Photo (top left) and choose either to take a photo with the iPhone's camera or choose an existing photo from the albums or camera roll already stored on the phone. Once you've selected an image, you can pinch and drag to frame the snap just the way you want it. When you're done, click Set Photo.

> **TIP: Adding pauses to phone numbers.** If you're adding a phone number that needs a pause at a certain stage – such as before a passcode or extension number – tap the # key, then tap Pause.

Contacts can...

Aside from making calls, contacts on the iPhone have several uses, including:

▶ Tap a contact's email address to instantly be presented with a blank email message addressed to that contact from your default account. For more on email, see p.181.

▶ Tap a contact's Web address listing to have the iPhone switch to Safari and take you straight to that webpage. For more on browsing the Web with an iPhone, see p.171.

▶ Tap a contact's address and the iPhone will show you the location in Maps. For more on Maps, see p.203.

> **TIP:** The listing for your own number is right under your nose but easy to miss. It's not buried in the Setting info but right at the top of the standard Contacts list.

07 Calls

From dialling to conference calling

Though the iPhone is special in many ways, it largely sticks to the familiar when it comes to making and receiving calls. This chapter whizzes you through the basics, offering some handy tips and tricks along the way.

Making calls

There are various different ways of making a call using the iPhone. Simply tap the Phone button, and then...

▶ Tap Contacts, pick a name and then choose a number (home, mobile, work, etc).

▶ Tap Keypad and type a number (hit ⌫ if you make a mistake). Then tap Call.

▶ To bring up and redial the last number you entered manually, tap Keypad, then Call.

▶ Tap Favorites and hit a name. Because each Favorite is a specific number, this saves you a couple of taps.

▶ To call someone you recently phoned, or who recently phoned you, click Recents and hit the relevant name or number.

> **TIP:** Even before your iPhone is activated or if it doesn't have a SIM card inserted, you can still call the emergency services. Tap Keypad and dial, for example, 911 in the US or 999 in the UK, then tap Call.

When you're on a call…

When the iPhone is close to your ear, the device's proximity sensor disables the screen, saving you power. However, move the phone away from your ear whilst on a call and the screen displays various call options:

▶ **Mute** When tapped, the caller can't hear you, but you can still hear them. Tap again to return to normal.

▶ **Add Call** For multiple and conference calls. See overleaf for more info.

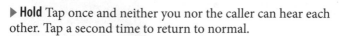

▶ **Keypad** Brings up the numeric keypad – essential when using automated phone systems.

▶ **Hold** Tap once and neither you nor the caller can hear each other. Tap a second time to return to normal.

▶ **Speaker** Toggles speaker-phone on and off. The iPhone's speaker is located on the base of the unit. As with other phones, the sound isn't amazing and may distort, in which case reduce the volume level using the buttons on the side of the iPhone.

Microphone   Speaker

▶ **Contacts** Takes you to your main Contacts list.

Multiple calls and conference calling

The iPhone has two lines available for calls. When you're talking to one person, you can click Add Call and dial someone else; the existing caller will be put on hold, and you can then use the Swap option to switch between the two lines. Likewise if someone calls you while you're on the phone, you'll be offered a Hold Call + Answer option.

Even better, the iPhone allows you to make conference calls with up to five people simultaneously. With a conference call, you don't need to switch between callers – everyone can be heard by everyone else. It works like this: one of the iPhone's two lines hosts the conference and the other is free to call people who can then be merged onto the conference line. And so on.

So, to get things started, make or receive a call in the usual way. Next, tap Add Call and dial someone else. The first call is put on hold while you do this so you can give the second person you've called warning that you want to add them to a conference – or, indeed, chat privately. Then, hit Merge Calls to create the three-way conversation. Follow the same procedure to add further callers to the party.

First caller (on hold)

Second caller (live)

Merge calls to start a conference

During a conference call, you can also…

▶ **Talk privately** with a particular caller. Tap Conference and then Private next to the relevant name. To bring both of you back to the conference, tap Merge.

▶ **Ditch a caller** Tap Conference, then tap End next to the relevant name.

▶ **Add an incoming call** Tap Hold Call + Answer and then Merge Calls.

And more...

While on a call, you can press the Home button to access any other applications without dropping your call – useful if you need to check a date in your calendar or an address in an email. Note, however, that you can only access the Internet during a call when you're connected to a Wi-Fi network (see p.59). So don't expect to use Safari or Maps while walking down the street in the middle of a conversation.

When you have finished with whatever it was you were doing, press the Home button again and then tap the green strip at the top of the screen to return to the Call Options screen.

Receiving calls

When someone calls you, the iPhone will either ring or vibrate (for set-ting up ringtones, etc, see p.54) and display the caller's information on the screen, including their photograph, if you have one set up in Contacts (see p.90). Next, do one of the following:

To answer a call

▶ Tap Answer or, if the iPhone is locked, drag the slider.

▶ If, when the call comes in, you have audio or video playing, it will fade out and pause. If you're using the supplied headset, click the headset's mic button.

To decline a call

If you don't want to talk, declining a call will send it straight to voicemail. This can be achieved either by tapping Decline on the screen, or:

▶ Pressing the Sleep/Wake button on the top of the iPhone twice in quick succession.

▶ If you are using the iPhone headset, press and hold the mic button for a couple of seconds, then let go. You will then hear two low beeps confirming that the call has been declined.

To silence a call

When a call comes in, you can quickly stop the iPhone ringing or vibrating without answering or declining the call – useful if, for instance, you get a personal call in the office and you want to step outside before answering it.

To do this, simply press the Sleep/Wake button or either of the volume buttons.

Sleep/Wake button

Volume buttons

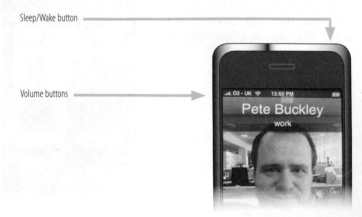

To answer a second call

If you have Call Waiting switched on, you can receive a second call while already on the phone. The iPhone will chirp in your ear, show the new caller information and offer you three options:

▶ **Ignore** Sends the new caller to voicemail.

▶ **End Call + Answer** Ends the call you were on and answers the new one.

▶ **Hold Call + Answer** Puts the first call on hold and answers the second. From there you can either switch between the two conversations using the Swap button or hit Merge to combine the calls into a three-way conference.

You can turn Call Waiting on and off within Settings, under the Phone sub-menu.

Recent and missed calls

Like other mobile phones, the iPhone keeps a list of recent incoming and outgoing calls. This can be used for reference – for example, showing you the time when someone phoned – or as a means of storing numbers or making calls. To access the list, tap Phone > Recents. Note that the Phone icon displays a small red circle containing the number of missed calls and unheard voicemails you have, and Recents boasts a similar circle only listing missed calls.

In the list, missed calls appear in red and can be viewed in isolation by tapping the Missed button. When a caller has attempted to reach you more than once, the number of missed calls is displayed in brackets.

Tapping  to the right of any entry will display more information about the call, such as whether it was incoming or outgoing. When a caller is already in your Contacts list, all their information is displayed, with the number that relates to that specific call highlighted in blue.

Visual Voicemail

One of the most revolutionary features of the iPhone is Visual Voicemail. The idea is that you no longer have to listen to all your voicemail messages in turn to get to the one you want. Instead, your voicemails are presented in a list – just like emails – and you can choose the ones you want to listen to in any order. You can even rewind and fast-forward. A few years from now we won't believe we ever did it any other way.

As mentioned, the Phone button on the Home screen displays a red circle containing the total number of missed calls and unheard voicemails.

Voicemail overseas

In some foreign countries, you may find that Visual Voicemail won't work. Instead, when you click Voicemail, you'll be offered a single Call Voicemail button which will take you through to your messages the old-fashioned way. As with other phones, you can also call your voicemail by holding down the 1 on the numeric keypad.

Tapping it reveals the Voicemail button, which also displays a red numbered icon, but this time just for unheard voicemails.

Voicemail setup

Tapping the Voicemail button for the first time takes you to a screen with an option to create a voicemail password, which you will use to access your voicemails from other phones (see p.101); you can change this password at any time from the iPhone's Settings screen, within the Phone sub-menu.

The first time you tap Voicemail, you'll also be prompted to record a greeting, which callers will hear prior to leaving you a message. Tap Greeting, then Custom, then Record. When you're done, you can play back your message and, if you're happy with it, tap Save. Alternatively, if you're feeling shy, you could tap Default instead of Custom and stick with the prerecorded greeting, which includes your number.

By default, the iPhone will alert you with a sound when you have a new voicemail (except if the Silent switch is on). If you'd rather turn this function off, tap Settings > Sounds and set the New Voicemail switch to Off.

> TIP: Messages are saved for thirty days from the time you first listen to them – regardless of whether or not you delete them.

Playback and more

The Voicemail screen lists current voicemail messages, with those you have not yet been listened to displaying a blue dot to their left. It is worth knowing that even though a voicemail appears in the list, it hasn't been downloaded to the phone. Thus, you need to have a network signal to listen to voicemails.

Each voicemail lets you...

▶ **Play/pause/rewind** You can play and pause a message at any time with the ▶ and ❚❚ icons. Even better, you can rewind or skip forward by dragging the scrubber bar. (One of the iPhone's finest moments in terms of innovation.)

▶ **Return a call** Tap the message and hit Call Back.

▶ **View details** Tapping the ⦿ button to the right of any message to find out the time and date it was recorded, its duration and the full contacts info of the caller, where known.

▶ **Contact the caller** Having tapped ⦿, you can tap the caller's number to call them, email address to send an email, or Text Message to send an SMS.

Voicemail list (a blue dot to the left denotes an unheard message)

Scrubber bar

▶ **Add to Contacts** Tap ⦿ next to a message and then Create New Contact, Add to Existing Contact or Add to Favorites.

Deleting and undeleting voicemails

One great thing about the iPhone's voicemail system is that deleted messages are saved for thirty days before being permanently erased.

▶ **To delete a message** Tap a message, then tap Delete.

▶ **To view deleted messages** Scroll to the bottom of the voicemail list and tap Deleted Messages.

▶ **To undelete a message** Choose a deleted message and click Undelete.

Picking up voicemail from another phone

You can pick up your iPhone voicemails the old-fashioned way using any phone. At least, American iPhone owners can; it remains to be seen if this will work in the UK or elsewhere.

Simply call your iPhone's number and, assuming it is not answered, you'll be redirected to your voicemail. When you hear your greeting, dial * followed by your voicemail password. Then enter # and follow the voice instructions.

Voicemail over speaker and Bluetooth

To listen to your voicemail messages over the iPhone's built-in speaker, tap the Speaker button in the top-right corner. Or, if your iPhone is connected to a Bluetooth headset or car kit (see p.217), tap Audio and choose Speaker Phone to use the built-in speaker. To switch back to the headset or car kit, tap Audio again, then choose the relevant device.

Other call features

Call Forwarding

If you'd like to have incoming calls forwarded to another number, click Settings, then Phone, then Call Forwarding and enter a number. This can be very handy if, for instance, you're going to be outside your network's coverage area but available on a landline.

Caller ID (outgoing)

If you'd like to call someone without your name or number flashing up on their phone screen, click Settings, then Phone, and switch off Show My Caller ID.

Super Caller ID

Tap a received call in your Recents list and you'll see a new screen with options for calling back, adding to contacts, etc. This page includes address details, when known, for callers already in your contacts list; for unknown callers, you'll see the area where the call came from. This "Super Caller ID" feature can be very handy when you receive a call with an unfamiliar area code. Unfortunately, the same info doesn't flash up when the phone actually rings.

Calling via the Internet

Anyone used to making calls via the Internet will be disappointed that the iPhone doesn't allow for the installation of programs such as Skype. If it did, you'd be able to make free or virtually free calls, locally and internationally, whenever you were connected to a Wi-Fi network.

Thankfully, all is not lost, for there are similar services that can be accessed via the Web. They enable you to make free or extremely inexpensive calls to landlines and mobiles in other countries. Since you don't need to install any software, they work fine with the iPhone.

Jajah

Sign up for a free Jajah account and you can call other Jajah users for free – even internationally – and make other long-distance calls at discounted rates (as little as 3¢/1.5p for the US, China and most of Westerm Europe). You go to the website using Safari and enter your own number and the number you want to call. Press

Go and your phone will ring; pick it up and the number you're calling will ring. Neither of you initiated the call, so neither of you will pay long-distance charges. You can even import your contact details from your phone to your personal Jajah page, via the Apple Address Book.

Jajah jajah.com

Rebtel

Rebtel works slightly differently to Jajah. Enter the phone number of a friend, relative or colleague in any of the fifty or so supported countries and Rebtel will give you a local number on which you can call using your free minutes, plus a tiny fee to Rebtel. Best of all, the numbers stick, so you can save one to your phone and use it whenever you want to call the same person.

The fees are as little as 1¢/1p per minute, but you can even avoid paying these if you like, by getting the person you're calling to phone you back on the number that shows up on their screen when you ring.

Rebtel rebtel.com

Calling an email address

Jangl offers a slightly different take on free Internet-based mobile-phone calls. Enter an email address of someone you know and Jangl will assign a number to that address. Dial this number and you can leave a voicemail for the person, who will receive it via email – wherever they are in the world. Or, if they're already a member, the call will divert to their nominated phone.

In addition, Jangl offers local-priced calls to around thirty countries, mainly in Europe and the Americas.

Jangl jangl.com

Calling from your computer

One advantage of being able to easily sync all your phone numbers from your phone to your computer is that you can then import them into an Internet telephony program and call the numbers from your computer in order to save your precious mobile minutes. For example, Skype, which is free to download, lets you import numbers from Address Book or Outlook. Just choose Import Contacts… in the Contacts menu.

Skype skype.com (PC & Mac)

Other programs that let you make cheap calls over the Internet to regular and mobile phones include:

AIM aim.com (PC & Mac)
Windows Live Messenger get.live.com/messenger (PC)
Yahoo! Messenger messenger.yahoo.com (PC & Mac)

To make decent-quality calls, your computer will need an audio headset or USB handset (pictured). It is possible to get by with a regular microphone and speakers (including those built into most laptops), but these tend to lead to annoying feedback and echoes because the sound from the speakers gets picked up by the microphone.

> TIP: When calling via the Internet, from a phone or a computer, you'll usually need to enter numbers complete with international dialling codes, even if you're not calling overseas. So it's good to get into the habit of using dialling codes when adding or editing contacts.

SMS

Texting by phone or computer

The iPhone is unprecedented in its incorporation of SMS, short for Single-Molecule Spectroscopy. OK, not really: the SMS application on the iPhone Home screen refers to Short Message Service – aka text messaging. It works just like on any other phone, expect that you get to use a full QWERTY keyboard and see your texts as threaded conversations – just as with chat tools such as iChat or Skype. Be warned, however, that despite this appearance, you're still using plain-old SMS messages, with each speech bubble in the conversation coming off your monthly message allocation.

Text alerts

When you have unread messages, the SMS icon on the Home screen will show a small red circle with a digit reflecting the number of new messages. If you also want the iPhone to play an alert sound when you get a text, tap Settings on the Home screen, then tap Sounds and use the New Text Message slider. (The sound won't play if the ringer button is switched to Silent.)

Texting

Clicking SMS reveals a list of new messages (signified by a blue dot) and existing "conversations". Tap an entry to view it and you're ready to reply. Alternatively:

▶ **To delete a message or conversation** Swipe left or right over it to reveal the Delete button. Alternatively, tap Edit, then ●.

▶ **To write a new message** tap ✉ and either enter a phone number, start typing the name of someone in your Contacts list to reveal a list of matching names, or hit ⊕ to browse for a contact. Annoyingly, you can't currently send single messages to multiple contacts, so party invites and the like are better dealt with using email.

▶ **To quickly send a text message to someone in your Favorites or Recents list** tap the ⊙ icon next to their name in the list and choose Text Message.

▶ **To call or email someone from your Text Messages list** tap a message in the list, scroll to the top of the conversation and tap Call or, to see their other numbers and email address, click Contact Info.

▶ **To add someone you've texted to your Contacts list** tap their phone number in the Text Messages list and then tap Add to Contacts.

> ▶ TIP: Street addresses, emails, weblinks or phone numbers in a text conversation can be tapped to launch Maps, Mail or Safari, or to start a call.

Chat and messaging

Though the iPhone doesn't offer any built-in tools for instant messaging – also known as chat – you can access all the common services via the Web. Just tap Safari and visit one of the following iPhone-optimized sites.

Sign in with your favorite network!

MSN
AIM
ICQ
Yahoo! (Coming soon!)
GTalk (Coming soon!)

©2007 Heysan Inc.

HeySan m.heysan.com
BeeJive iphone.beejive.com
PhoneIM foneim.com

HeySan and BeeJive offer (or will soon offer) access to AIM, Google Talk, iChat, ICQ, MSN and Yahoo!. PhoneIM works with Google Talk and Jabber. Once logged in to your network of choice, you can chat with people on computers in addition to those on their phones. It's global, instant and free.

One of the most popular multi-network chat programs for computers is Trillian, the creators of which are soon to launch an iPhone-optimized service called Astra. Not just a chat program, Astra promises to tie together all kinds of online activity and "change your Web". It will be interesting to see if it lives up to its own hype...

Trillian Astra ceruleanstudios.com

Texting from your computer

Though we're used to sending SMS messages from our phones, it's also possible to do so from a computer. This can be a great way to save money and make the SMS allocation on your iPhone's monthly plan go further.

Various websites allow you to send free SMS messages – in many cases, go to the carrier website of the person you want to text and enter your message there. But it's also possible to send free text messages – to US numbers at least – from most chat applications.

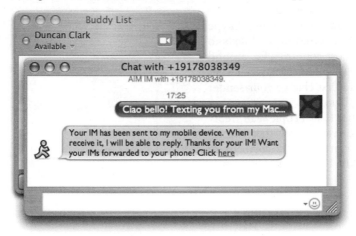

> TIP: A little-known feature of the Mac Address Book is its ability to pair with a Bluetooth phone (using the third button on the toolbar) and then send SMS messages via the phone, giving you the advantage of a real-world keyboard. Just click "Mobile" and choose SMS message. It remains to be seen if this feature will be added to the iPhone, which currently can't communicate with a Mac via Bluetooth.

In AOL Instant Messenger or iChat, for instance, just create a new message from the File menu and enter the recipient's mobile number where you'd usually enter a "screen name". You'll need to include +1 at the beginning, as SMS messages sent through the Internet require a country code.

Texting internationally

If you want to text someone in a foreign country, but don't want to pay international rates via your mobile plan, you can use Skype (see p.105) to send texts to most countries for around 8¢/5p. However, you'll want to first change your sender ID to your iPhone number so that people can reply directly. Note that the ID won't show up correctly in the US, China or Taiwan.

iPod

09 Music

...on iTunes & on the iPhone

The Apple iPhone is a fully functional iPod. In fact, it's actually better than other iPods, since it benefits from a bigger screen and various extra features such as Cover Flow, which lets you browse through your music collection by flicking through album artwork.

As with all other iPods, the iPhone is designed as a music *player* rather than a music *manager*. You download tracks, import CDs or vinyl, add artwork and generally keep things in good order in iTunes rather than on the iPhone itself.

As such, the first half of this chapter explains how to use iTunes effectively. The second half deals with music on the iPhone.

Stocking up your iTunes Library

To get music onto your iPhone, you first have to get it onto your computer. There are various ways to do this: import CDs; download from iTunes or other stores; import existing music files; or even record from vinyl or audio cassette. Let's take a look at each of these in turn…

Option 1: Import from CD

To get music from a CD onto your iPhone, you simply import – or "rip" – the disc into your iTunes Library, and the tracks will be ready to transfer to your iPhone next time you hook it up. To get started, insert the CD and it will appear on the Source List on the left of the iTunes window.

Downloading and editing track names

No track name information is stored in a standard audio CD. Rather, when you put a disc in to your computer, iTunes examines the contents and downloads the relevant track info via the Internet from CDDB – a giant database hosted by a company called Gracenote (gracenote.com). For that reason, the track names will only appear when you're connected to the Internet. If you don't have an always-on Internet connection, insert the CD, connect to the Internet and then select Get CD Track Names from the Advanced menu in iTunes.

If iTunes can't find the track names, the songs will be left with the titles "Track 1", "Track 2" and so on. This is rare, but it's highly likely that the info downloaded may either be inaccurate or won't tally with your own ideas of music categorization – one person's hip-hop is another's R&B, after all. In either case, you'll need to edit the information manually either before or after importing the CD. See p.135 for more information.

Joining tracks

Before importing the tracks from a CD it's possible to "join" some of them together. Then, when they're played back on your computer or your iPod, they'll always stay together as one unit, and iTunes won't insert a gap between the tracks. This is useful if you have an album in which two or more tracks are segued together or if you just think certain tracks should always be heard together, even in Shuffle mode.

Simply select the tracks you want to join and then click Join CD Tracks from the Advanced menu. In the short term you can change your mind by clicking Unjoin CD Tracks, but once you've pressed Import, the songs will be imported as a single audio file that cannot be separated without the use of audio-editing software.

▲	Song Name
1	☑ ┌ Mara
2	Timo Ma
3	Phaser
4	Danny T
5	Sandra C
6	└ Stef

Importing...

To the left of each song title you'll see a check box; if you don't wish to import a particular track from a CD, uncheck its box. Finally, hit the Import CD button in the lower right-hand corner of the iTunes window and watch as each of your selections is copied to your hard drive.

> TIP: It's fine to mix different file formats and bitrates in your Library. If you're a hi-fi buff with plenty of computer disk space, consider importing your CDs using Apple Lossless for use through your stereo but creating an AAC copy of each for use on your iPhone, where disk space is more limited. After you've created the copies, simply create a Smart Playlist (see p.141) that finds all MP3 and AAC files, and set your iPhone to automatically update that playlist only (see p.143).

Music file formats and bitrates

Before importing lots of CDs, make sure you're happy with the file format and sound-quality settings. You don't want to have to re-rip all your CDs a few months down the line if you decide that you're not happy with the sound, or you want to use the tracks with an MP3 player that doesn't support Apple's default file formats. To access the iTunes Importing options, open iTunes Preferences, click the Advanced button and choose the Importing tab. The two most important options are file format (labelled Import Using) and bitrate (labelled Setting).

Which file format?

Music can be saved in various different file formats, just like images (bitmap, jpeg, gif, etc) and text documents (doc, txt, rtf, etc) can be. When you import a CD to iTunes, you can pick from AAC, MP3, **Apple Lossless**, Wav and Aiff. Here's the lowdown on each:

MP3 [Moving Pictures Experts Group-1/2 Audio Layer 3]
Pros: Compatible with all MP3 players and computer systems. Allows you to burn high-capacity CDs for playback on MP3-capable CD players.
Cons: Not quite as good as AAC in terms of sound quality per megabyte.
File name ends: .mp3

AAC [Advanced Audio Coding]
Pros: Excellent sound quality for the disk space it takes up.
Cons: Not compatible with much non-Apple hardware or software.
File name ends: .m4a (or .m4p for protected files from the iTunes Store)

Apple Lossless Encoder
Pros: Full CD sound quality in half the disk space of an uncompressed track.
Cons: Files are still very large and only play back on iTunes, iPhones and iPods.
File name ends: .ale

AIFF/Wav
Pros: Full CD sound quality. Plays back on any system.
Cons: Huge files.
File name ends: .aiff/.wav

Which bitrate?

The bitrate is the amount of data used to encode each second of sound. Higher bitrates make for better sound quality but also use more disk space. For instance, a track encoded at a bitrate of 128 kbps takes half as much space as the same track recorded at 256 kbps.

The default import setting in recent versions of iTunes is AAC at 128 kbps. Most people will be perfectly satisfied with this combination (which is usually said to be roughly equivalent to MP3 at 160 kbps), but if you're into your sound in a serious way it may not be good enough. In particular, if you listen to high-fidelity recordings of acoustic instruments and if you connect your iPhone or computer to a decent home stereo, you may sense a lack of presence and brightness. If so, either opt for the Apple Lossless Encoder or stick with AAC and up the bitrate. Note, however, that the iPhone won't play AAC or MP3 files at bitrates above 320 kbps.

Converting one music file format to another

iTunes allows you to create copies of imported tracks in different file formats. This is great for reducing the size of bulky WAV, AIFF or Apple Lossless files, or for creating MP3 versions of songs that you want to give to friends who have non-Apple music players or phones. Be warned, however, that re-encoding one compressed file format (such as AAC) into another (such as MP3) will damage the sound quality somewhat.

To create a copy of a track in a different format, first specify your desired format and bitrate on the iTunes Importing Preferences panel under Advanced. Then close Preferences, select the file or files in question and choose Convert selection to… from the Advanced menu.

Note that you can't convert tracks downloaded from stores such as iTunes. However, it is usually possible to burn them to CD and then re-rip them in a different format instead. Note, though, this may break the terms of your user licence, depending on where you got the track.

Stereo Bit Rate:	160 kbps ⬧
	☐ Use Variable Bit Rate Encoding (VBR)
Quality:	Highest ⬧
(With VBR enabled, bit rate settings are used for a guaranteed minimum bit rate.)	
Sample Rate:	Auto ⬧
Channels:	Stereo ⬧
Stereo Mode:	Joint Stereo ⬧
	☑ Smart Encoding Adjustments
	☑ Filter Frequencies Below 10 Hz

Tweaking the settings

When setting the bitrate, "Custom" reveals a panel full of extra settings, such as Variable Bit Rate and Sample Rate. These are usually best left as they are, though the mono option can be useful for saving disk space if importing non-stereo recordings.

Option 2: Downloading from iTunes

The iTunes Store offers instant, legal access to over five million tracks for as little as 79p/99¢ each. It's not a website as such: the only way in is through the iTunes software. Simply click the Music Store icon in the Source List, and after a few seconds the iTunes window will be taken over by the Store's front page.

Navigating

You shouldn't struggle to find your way around the iTunes Store. Like online CD stores such as Amazon, it lets you peruse by genre, look at "Staff Favorites", "Featured Artists", "Exclusives" and so on. But it also lets you use the various tools – such as the Search box and Browse function – familiar from browsing your own iTunes Library. The homepage also features a link to "Power Search" where you can narrow your search criteria.

You can go "up a level", or right back to the Store's homepage, by clicking the tabs at the top right.

Quicklinks

Whether you are browsing your own Library or the Music Store's catalogue, you can use the grey circular Quicklink buttons in the Song List to quickly access all the iTunes Store's selections for a particular artist. Quicklinks can be turned on and off for your own Library in iTunes Preferences under General.

> TIP: If you want to quickly see all the music and video you ever purchased from the iTunes Music Store, click "Check for purchases…" in the iTunes Store menu or click the green Purchases icon in the Source list.

Previewing music

You can preview thirty seconds' worth of any track within the Music Store catalogue simply by double-clicking the song's name in the Song List. You can also drag any previews into playlists on the Source List to listen to later. These previews will appear in the Song List all ready for you to click when you want to buy the whole track.

DRM restrictions and iTunes Plus

Since the launch of the iTunes Store, the standard music files offered have been encoded at 128 kbps and included digital rights management (DRM) protection that imposes certain limitations on how you can use the files. The limitations include:

▸ The tracks aren't playable on non-Apple software or hardware.

▸ Downloads from your account can only be "authorized" to play on five computers at any one time. This way Apple hope that they can curb the unauthorized sharing of copyrighted music. Your computer is authorized to play music you purchase when you set up your account, or when you enter your ID and password to play a song that you've downloaded. If your account is already authorized with five computers, you will have to deauthorize one of the machines before playing any of the tracks on a sixth. This is done by selecting Deauthorize computer… from the Store menu in iTunes. If you ever plan to sell or ditch an old machine which has been used to play purchased songs, make sure you deauthorize it first.

▸ You can burn individual purchased songs to CD as many times as you like, but you can only burn a playlist seven times if it contains purchased songs. (You can always recompile the playlist if you really need to burn the selections again.)

You can get around these restrictions by burning tracks to CD and then re-ripping them, but it's a hassle and won't do the sound quality any good. Another alternative is to purchase tracks from the iTunes Plus section of the store. These tracks are higher sound quality – encoded at 256 kbps – and don't have any in-built limitations. Note, though, that they're still AAC files (see p.116), so they'll only play on non-Apple software and hardware which support that file format, unless you convert them to MP3 (see p.117).

Buying music

You will have setup an account with the store when you setup your iPhone for the first time, so you should have a username and password ready to go.

There are two ways to buy tracks. You could use the "1-Click" method, whereby a single click of a Buy Song button in the Song

List will debit the payment from your card and start the track downloading to your iTunes Library. Alternatively you can shop using a "Shopping Cart", which appears in the Source List. As you browse the store you add songs to your cart using the Add Song buttons; when you are done, click the cart's icon in the Source List, inspect its contents and then hit the Buy Now button in the bottom-right corner to pay and start downloading.

You can set which method you wish to use in the iTunes Preferences panel – look under the Store tab.

> **TIP:** If you want to stop your kids either accessing the Music Store entirely or having their tender ears exposed to explicit material, look for the options under the Parental tab of iTunes Preferences.

More in the Store

▶ **Publish an iMix** The iTunes Store gives you the option of publishing your playlists so that others can either draw inspiration from (or snigger at) your impeccable taste. Note, though, that only songs available in the Music Store will be listed. To publish a playlist, select it in the Source List and choose Create an iMix… from the File menu. To email a friend with the link to your published mix, click the arrow button to the right of the published playlist in the Source List and click "Tell a friend".

▶ **Giving music** You can buy and send "Gift Certificates" as well as prepaid "iTunes Music Cards" that can be redeemed in the Store. The link is on the homepage with full instructions. Here you'll also see a link for setting up a "Monthly Gift" allowance account: you authorize someone to spend a set amount of money each month that is then charged to your credit card.

▶ **Billboard charts** If you are a patron of the US iTunes Music Store there is also a link on the homepage to the Billboard charts, and not just their current listing, but also hit parades from years gone by. These can be a useful resource. European shoppers can browse the US Store via the dropdown menu at the bottom of the homepage.

▶ **Freebies** Keep an eye open for free tracks: you get something for nothing, and you might discover an artist you never knew you liked. Also on offer are free-to-stream music videos, though you'll need a fast Internet connection to make them worth watching.

Option 3: Other download services

Though it's the obvious choice for iTunes users, the iTunes Store doesn't hold all the cards when it comes to selling music online. There are many other services out there – some are less expensive, others offer tracks that iTunes doesn't, and some even donate their profits to charity.

iTunes' biggest competitors – such as Napster – offer DRM-protected WMA files that currently won't play back in iTunes or on an iPhone. However, there are various services that offer plain old MP3 files. These tend to be specialists in music from indie labels, which are more relaxed about allowing their music to be distributed in an unprotected format. These include the following:

AudioLunchbox audiolunchbox.com
A top-class selection from independent labels. Most tracks are 99¢, though there are freebies to be had too.

Bleep bleep.com
Electronica and indie, including everything from the Warp Records catalogue and loads more. You can preview whole tracks before buying, at which point expect to pay 99p per song or £6.99 for an album.

eMusic emusic.com
Perhaps the main competitor to iTunes for iPod owners, this brilliant service offers 600,000 songs from indie labels. For $9.99 per month you get 40 tracks – which works out at only ¢25 per track.

Epitonic epitonic.com
Insound insound.com/mp3
Freebies from underground and independent artists. Mostly American.

IntoMusic intomusic.co.uk
Indie and alternative stuff for 60p per track. There are subscription and buy-in-bulk payment options for keen users.

Matador Records matadorrecords.com
Free offerings from the label whose roster includes Cat Power and Mogwai.

Mperia mperia.com
A space where unsigned artists can sell, or give away, their music. They keep 70 percent of anything you pay.

PlayLouder playlouder.com
PlayLouder is at present a music site with a decent selection of MP3s at 99p each (£7.99 max for an album). However, look out for this name, as they

have recently launched playlouderMSP.com, the first legal file-sharing network, which could quite easily redefine the way we download music in the future.

Sub Pop Records subpop.com
Free tracks from the label who brought us Nirvana and others.

Vitaminic vitaminic.com
Unsigned artists of variable quality. Tracks range from free to 99p, with unlimited access at $40 for six months.

Wippit wippit.com
Though some of the bigger-name tracks are only available as iPod-unfriendly WMA files, Wippit also offers loads of MP3s – starting at only 29p each. Subscription options also available.

Calabash Music calabashmusic.com
World Music served up according to fair-trade principles.

Download.com Music music.download.com
Free music by amateur or up-and-coming artists. It's the archive that used to live at MP3.com – now a site that lets you compare (and search for tracks across) the major music services.

Russian services

In between the legit and the illegit, there are MP3 websites that are, well, kind of legal. All Of MP3, for example, is the best known of the Russian sites which use a loophole in their country's broadcast law to openly offer a huge download archive without permission from the labels. They offer all formats and bitrate "by the weight" – you buy, say, 100MB for a comparatively tiny fee. It's left up to you to ensure you don't break the law of your own country when downloading.

All Of MP3 allofmp3.com

Option 4: Importing music files

As well as getting music into your iTunes library by ripping your CDs or purchasing online, you can also import music files from other locations on your computer or connected storage devices, such as hard drives or flash drives. Simply browse for the files, or folders of files, you want to import and drag them straight into the main iTunes window (or onto a specific playlist icon if you like). The same thing can be achieved by choosing the Add to Library command from the File menu and then pointing to the relevant file or folder.

To make sure you're actually *copying* the files into your iTunes library – rather than simply importing them from their current location – open iTunes Preferences before you start importing and click the Advanced button. Under the General tab make sure that the "Copy files to iTunes Music folder when adding to library" box is checked. Now, after you have imported your songs you can delete the original files from your computer, safe in the knowledge that they have been copied to your iTunes Music folder.

Option 5: Recording from vinyl or cassette

If you have the time and inclination, it's perfectly possible to import music from analogue sound sources such as vinyl, cassette or radio into iTunes and onto your iPhone. For vinyl, the easiest option is to buy a USB turntable, such as those from Ion or Kam (pictured), but this isn't strictly necessary. With the right cables, you can connect your hi-fi, Walkman, minidisc player or any other source to your computer and do it manually.

Hooking up

First of all, you'll need to make the right connection. With any luck, your computer will have a line-in or mic port, probably in the form of a minijack socket (if it doesn't you can add one with the right USB device; ask in any computer store). On the hi-fi, a headphone socket will suffice, but you'll get a much better "level" from a dedicated line-out – check on the back of the system for a pair of RCA sockets labelled "Line Out", "Tape Out" or something similar. Depending on whether you're connecting to a headphone jack or a pair of RCA sockets, you'll either need minijack-to-minijack cable or an RCA-to-minijack cable (see p.222).

Check you have enough disk space

During the actual recording process, you'll need plenty of hard-drive space: as much as a gigabyte for an album, or 15MB per minute. Once you've finished recording, you can convert the music that you've imported into a space-efficient format such as MP3 or AAC, and delete the giant originals.

Choose some software

Recording from an analogue source requires an audio editing application. You may already have something suitable on your computer, but there are also scores of excellent programs available to download off the Internet. Our recommendations would be GarageBand (pictured overleaf) for Mac users, which anyone with an Apple machine purchased in the last few years will already have, and Audacity (pictured below), which is available for both PC and Mac, is easy to use and totally free:

Audacity audacity.sourceforge.net
GarageBand apple.com/garageband

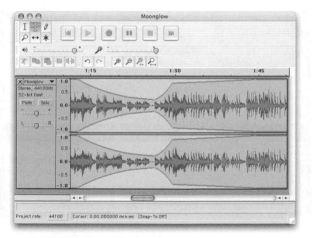

Recording...

Connect your computer and hi-fi as described above, and switch your hi-fi's amplifier to "Phono", "Tape" or whichever channel you're recording from. Launch your audio recorder and open a new file. The details from here on in vary according to which program you're running and the analogue source you are recording from, but roughly speaking the procedure is the same.

You'll be asked to specify a few parameters for the new recording. The defaults (usually 44.1kHz, 16-bit stereo) should be fine. Play the loudest section of the record to get an idea of the maximum level. A visual meter should display the sound coming in – you want as much level as possible *without* hitting the red.

If you seem to be getting little or no level, make sure your line-in is specified as your recording channel and the input volume is up: on a Mac, look under Sound in System Preferences; on a PC, look in Control Panel.

When you're ready, press "Record" and start your vinyl, cassette or other source playing. When the song or album is finished, press

"Stop". A graphic wave form will appear on the screen. Use the "cut" tool to tidy up any extraneous noise or blank space from the beginning and end of the file; fade in and out to hide the "cuts", and, if you like, experiment with any hiss, pop and crackle filters on offer.

Drop it into iTunes

When you are happy with what you've got, save the file in WAV or AIFF format, import it into iTunes (choose Import… from the File menu), convert it to AAC or MP3 (see p.117) and delete the bulky original from both your iTunes folder and its original location.

> **TIP:** If you use GarageBand, you can export directly to iTunes from the Share menu. Before doing so, choose a sound quality by opening Preferences and looking within the Export tab.

Managing music in iTunes

Searching

The Search box, on the right-hand side at the top of the iTunes environment, lets you find a track by typing all or part of the name of the artist, album, track title or composer. You can
search more than one field at once, so typing *Bee Vio*, for example, would bring up Beethoven's Violin Concerto.

Note that iTunes will only search those tracks currently showing in the Song List. So if you want to search your whole collection, make sure that the Music icon is selected in the Source List, and "All" is selected in the Genre column before you start to type.

Browsing

iTunes offers three view modes to help you browse through your music: list, grouped with artwork, and Cover Flow, which lets you "flick through" your virtual album sleeves. (For tips on stocking up with album artwork,
see p.138.) Explore these using the three buttons adjacent to the Search box.

In the first two modes, also try out the Browser tool, which you'll find in the View menu. This essential feature displays your collection by genre, artist and album. Clicking an entry under Genre reveals the artists from that genre; clicking an entry under Artists, in turn, reveals all the albums of that artist. And, with

> **TIP:** You'll probably be using the Browser tool a lot, so for quick access get used to the relevant keyboard shortcuts: Apple+B (Mac) or Ctrl+B (PC).

each selection, the Song List changes to display only the relevant songs. You'll find a couple of options for Browse mode under the General pane of iTunes Preferences. Here, you can turn the Genre column on and off, and also specify whether you want albums that are tagged as compilations to appear within the Artist column.

Columns and sorting

When browsing a list of songs in iTunes, you'll see various columns such as Artist, Album, etc. Clicking on a column header will sort the tracks by that category.

You can add and remove columns at any time using the View Options box, which can be summoned from the Edit menu or with the shortcut Apple+J (Mac) or Ctrl+J (PC). Alternatively, try Ctrl-clicking (Mac) or right-clicking (PC) the header of any of the columns in the Song List to reveal a dropdown menu of columns.

Once you've checked all the columns you want to see, and unchecked those you don't, your Song List should change to reflect this. But that's not all. You can then rearrange the columns – by dragging their headers – into any order you want.

Shuffle & repeat

In its default state, iTunes will play whatever is in the Song List, in the order shown in the Song List, and then stop. But there are various other options, accessible via the Controls menu or via the buttons at the bottom of the iTunes window.

▶ **Repeat** Select Repeat All and whatever is currently in the Song List will loop forever. Select Repeat One and only the track currently playing will loop.

▶ **Shuffle** With Shuffle turned on, iTunes plays the contents of the Song List in random order.

> TIP: When Shuffle is on, you can see what's coming next by clicking the top of the track number column. If you don't like the order selected, reshuffle by holding down Alt (Mac) or Shift (PC) and clicking the Shuffle button.

More shuffling

Though there's no such thing as true random-order generation, computers do an excellent job of simulating genuine disorder. But ever since the early days of iTunes and iPods, users have complained of a distinct presence of pattern, even predictability, in the "random" selections generated by the Shuffle mode. Perhaps it's just superstition – no one outside Apple HQ seems to know how Shuffle actually works – but people claim to hear certain artists or tunes appearing more than others, and genres or artists appearing in chunks rather than evenly spread out.

iTunes 5 improved things with the introduction of Smart Shuffle, which lets you choose from a sliding scale of randomness, from "more likely" (related songs and genres will tend to follow each other) to "less likely" (expect decidedly odd juxtapositions). Furthermore, you can now choose to have your Shuffle mode proceed by whole albums or groupings instead of individual songs. You'll find these options in iTunes under Preferences, under Playback and on an iPhone you'll find a Shuffle option at the top of any Song List.

In iTunes, you can avoid tracks repeating by creating a Smart Playlist (see p.141) for songs which have a Play Count of less than, say, two. When the music finally stops, change the Play Count setting to 3. And so on.

One final Shuffle tip: if you don't want a specific track to appear in any Shuffle selections, highlight the track, press Get Info in the File menu and, under Options, select "Skip when shuffling".

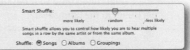

Party Shuffle, found in the iTunes Source List, is a play mode that generates a random mix of tracks drawn from either a playlist of your choice or your entire Library. When Party Shuffle is being used, a new panel appears at the bottom of the Song List, in which you can set parameters for how the list looks and where the tracks are drawn from, though you can also add selections from anywhere in your Library by dragging them onto the Party Shuffle icon in the Source List. At any time you can regenerate the track list either manually – by dragging them up and down – or automatically – by hitting the Refresh button in the top right corner of the iTunes window (this will replace the list's contents with fresh selections, but not remove manually added songs). If you don't want to see the Party Shuffle icon in the Source List, you can choose to hide it by unchecking the box under the General settings in iTunes Preferences.

Deleting music from iTunes

When deleting music from iTunes, first make sure that Library is selected in the Source List. If a playlist is selected instead, the tracks will be deleted from that list but not from iTunes itself. Next, select whichever songs, albums, artists or genres you want to delete and either…

▶ **Hit Backspace or Delete** on your keyboard.

▶ **Select Clear** from the Edit menu (or right-click menu).

▶ **Drag the selections to the Trash** (Mac only).

If asked, opt to send the files to the Trash, otherwise they'll remain in your iTunes folder, taking up space unnecessarily.

> TIP: If you want to remove something from iTunes but *not* delete it from your computer, first drag the file from iTunes onto your Desktop. Then delete the track from iTunes in the normal way.

Show me the music

Unless you change the settings, each imported or downloaded song is saved as an individual file in a hierarchy of folders which reside within your iTunes folder. This can be found within either your Music folder (Mac) or My Documents folder (PC). The hierarchy is defined by the artist and album information of each track. For example, The Beatles' "Dig A Pony" can be tracked down via: **iTunes ▶ iTunes Music ▶ The Beatles ▶ Let It Be ▶ Dig A Pony**

Housekeeping: adding and editing track info

As your iTunes library fills up, it might start to become a bit messy. You might find, for instance, certain artists and genres listed under two different names – "N Cave" & "Nick Cave", for instance, or R&B and R'n'B. You may also find that some tracks have certain bits of information missing. This is annoying, can make songs harder to find, and stops Smart Playlists working effectively. So it's worth taking the time to tidy up occasionally.

You can enter song information directly in the iTunes window by clicking on a track twice – not too quickly. Any existing text will become highlighted and you're ready to type. When you're done, hit Enter.

Alternatively, to view, add or edit all kinds of information about a track, select it in the Song List and choose Get Info from the File menu – or use the keyboard shortcut Apple+I (Mac) or Ctrl+I (PC). You can also edit information about multiple songs simultaneously by clicking on them while holding down Apple or Control, or by selecting entire artists, genres or albums in the Browser view (see p.130). Alongside the obvious bits of information, such as Artist, Title and Genre, you'll find various other fields, such as the following, all of which can be useful when creating Smart Playlists (see p.141).

▶ **Comment** For whatever additional info you like: personnel, producer, instruments used, even lyrics.

▶ **Grouping** Another wild-card category. World music fans might enter a country, say, or classical fans might enter a century.

iTunes EQ and volume settings

iTunes offers various ways to tweak the sound of your music files during playback. None will make as much difference as a decent pair of earphones or speakers, but they're definitely worth exploring.

Equalizer

The iTunes graphic equalizer tool can be either turned on or off as you listen or applied to individual tracks. You can access Equalizer via its stripy button in the lower right corner of the iTunes window. (This button also tells you whether Equalizer is currently active by glowing blue.) From the dropdown menu you can choose between a number of preset frequency settings, such as "Dance" (with heavy bass) or "Spoken Word" (with stronger mid-range frequencies).

At any time you can drag the sliders up and down yourself to try and get a better balance. If you create an EQ that you like, you can save it by selecting "Make Preset…" from the dropdown and choosing a name. It then becomes available in the list with the others.

To assign a preset to a specific track, select the song in question, choose "Get Info" from

> TIP: You can create your own genres rather than sticking
> with those in the list. If you mainly listen to jazz, say,
> you might want to use "bebop", "modal" and so on.

▶ **My Rating** This is where you get to play music reviewer and
enter a 0–5 star rating of each song.

▶ **BPM** Lets you specify the beats per minute of a track, which
can be used to create DJ-style mixes – either manually or by
sort a playlist by BPM and turning on the "Crossfade" feature in

the File menu and, under Options, look for the Equalizer Preset dropdown.
These settings will be carried over to the iPhone when you sync, but it's also
possible to apply an Equalizer Preset on the iPhone itself – look within the
Settings menu.

Sound Enhancer
Sound Enhancer, which you'll
find within the Playback pane
of iTunes Preferences, aims
to improve the "presence" of
compressed digital music files,
making it sound brighter and
more vivid. You may not like
the effect – or not be able to

tell the difference – but it's worth experimenting with, so check the box, slide
the slider and see what you think.

Volume settings
If you want to boost or lower the volume of a particular track for playback
on iTunes and the iPhone, select it, choose Get Info from the File menu,
hit Options and use the Volume Adjustment slider. Alternatively, try Sound
Check, found within the Playback pane of iTunes Preferences or the Settings
menu within the iPhone. With this tool activated, iTunes attempts to play
back songs at roughly the same volume level.

the Preferences/Playback. If you're a musician, this tag may also come in handy for picking songs to sample.

▶ **Start/stop times** Lets you top or tail tracks to remove annoying beginnings or endings – applause, indulgent band banter, etc.

Adding album art

Downloads from iTunes come with cover artwork, but the rest of your collection may be lacking in this department. Thankfully, iTunes now offers a tool for sorting this out; hit Get Album Artwork in the Advanced menu, and iTunes will find, download and apply as many album sleeves as it can.

Unless you're lucky, however, there will still be gaps. These can usually be plugged by looting images from the Internet. Search

Clicking the fourth button below the Source List reveals/hides the artwork panel; clicking the title bar of the panel toggles between showing artwork for the Selected Song and Now Playing song

iTunes sharing over a network

If more than one computer is connected to a network (ie sharing an Internet connection), then each computer can access the music on the others. First, Open iTunes Preferences (see p.45) and, under the Sharing tab, you'll see two main checkboxes: "Look for shared music" and "Share my music". You can also add a password, if you like.

Once that's done, icons for each computer will appear in the others' Source List in the left of the iTunes window. When you've finished with someone else's Library you "eject" it in the same way that you do a CD or your iPhone: either hit the icon to the right of the shared music icon in the Source List, or hit the eject button in the bottom right of the iTunes window.

Google Images or major CD stores and you should find what you're after. If not, you could always scan real-world album covers or simply use a difference images – such as a photos of the artist.

Once you've found an image you want to use – preferably a decently sized version rather than a thumbnail – drag it to your Desktop. Next, open iTunes and reveal the image panel by clicking View Artwork in the View menu. Select the track or tracks in question and drag the image into the panel.

> **TIP:** It's also possible to paste images into the image panel, or to choose Get Info from the File menu and point iTunes to the file. Mac users can even drag images straight from Safari into the iTunes artwork panel.

Visualizer

iTunes Visualizer is a psychedelic light show that swirls and morphs in time with the music. Depending on your taste, it will either hypnotize you into a state of blissful paralysis or – more likely – annoy the hell out of you. The Visualizer can be turned on or off by clicking its button in the bottom right corner of the iTunes window (the one with the flower-like icon). There's also a Visualizer menu where you can set how large you want the visuals to appear in the iTunes window and enable or disable the full-screen mode, with which the swirling patterns take over your whole monitor, just like a screen saver.

When the Visualizer is doing its thing, the button in the top right corner of the iTunes window can be used to open the Options pane.

Playlists

A key pillar of the digital music era is the playlist: a homemade combination of tracks for playing on your computer or iPhone; for burning to CD; for sending to friends; or even for publishing online. Like the old-fashioned mix tape, a playlist can be made for a particular time, place or person, or just for fun. Unlike cassettes, however, playlists can be created instantly; they can be as long as you like; they won't have poor sound quality; and there's no need to buy physical media.

The first thing to understand about playlists is that they don't actually contain any music files. All they contain is a list of pointers to tracks within your iTunes Library. This means you can delete playlists, and individual tracks within them, without deleting the actual music files. Likewise, you can add the same track to as many playlists as you like without using up extra disk space.

Creating playlists

To create a new playlist, either hit the New Playlist button (the +) at the bottom-left of the iTunes window or press Apple+N (Mac) or Ctrl+N (PC). A new playlist icon will appear, ready to be named and filled. You can drag songs onto the icon individually, or select a whole artist, album or genre in Browser mode and copy that across in one fell swoop.

You can also create a new playlist by dragging songs, artists, albums or genres directly into some blank space at the end of the Source List.

Rearranging, renaming and deleting playlists

You can sort the contents of a playlist automatically by clicking the top of each column in the Song List (artist, album, etc). Or, to sort them manually, first sort by the number column and then drag the tracks at will.

To rename a playlist, click its name once and then again (not too fast). To delete one, highlight it and press the backspace key; select Clear from the Edit or right-click menus; or, on a Mac, drag the icon into the Trash.

Smart Playlists

Smart Playlists are just like normal playlists but, rather than being compiled manually by you, iTunes does the work on your behalf, collecting all tracks in your Library that fulfil a set of rules, or "conditions", that you define. It might be songs that have a certain word in their title, or a set of genres, or the tracks you listened to the most – or a combination of any of these kinds of things. The

clever thing about Smart Playlists is that their contents will automatically change over time, as relevant tracks are added to your Library or existing tracks meet the criteria by being, say, rated highly.

To create a new Smart Playlist, look in the File menu or click the New Playlist button while holding down Alt (Mac) or Shift (PC) – you'll see the plus sign change into a cog. This will open the Smart

Smart Playlist ideas

Following are a few examples to give you an idea of the kinds of things you can do with Smart Playlist. For more inspiration, check out smartplaylists.com.

Functional...

Tracks I've never heard
▶ Play Count is 0
Lets you hear music that you've ripped or downloaded but not yet played.

On the up
▶ Date Added is in the last 60 days
▶ My Rating is greater than 3 stars
▶ Play Count is less than 5
A playlist of new songs that deserve more of a listen.

...or inspirational

A compilation of questions
▶ Song Name contains "?"
For days with no answers.

Space songs
▶ Song Name contains "space"
▶ Song Name contains "stars"
▶ Song Name contains "moon"
▶ Song Name contains "rocket"
For those who love their sci-fi as much as their music.

Playlist box, where you set the parameters for the new list. Simply click + and – to add and remove rules. It's a bit like a bizarre kind of musical algebra.

To edit the rules of an existing Smart Playlist, select it and choose Edit Smart Playlist in the File menu – or in the menu you get by right-clicking (PC) or Ctrl-clicking (Mac).

Playlist folders

Once you've amassed scores of playlists, you may find it useful to keep them organized in folders. You'll find the option to create a folder within the File menu. Once you've created one, you can simply drag playlists – or even other folders – into it.

Putting music on the iPhone

Getting your iTunes collection onto your iPhone is simple. Connect the phone and select its icon on the left of the iTunes windows. Under the Music tab, check the box to sync your music and then choose whether you'd prefer to have all your music copied across to the phone or just either sync all your music or just specific playlists.

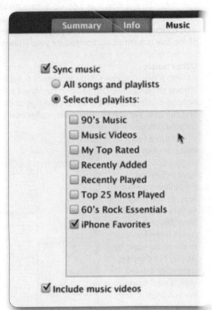

If you try to sync more music than can be fitted into the available space on your iPhone, iTunes will ask if you want to create a playlist of the appropriate size and set it to sync with the iPhone. If you answer yes, iTunes will randomly fill a new playlist which you can add to and remove from in the usual way.

Build your own playlist

A good alternative to using the automatically generated iPhone playlist is to create your own Smart Playlist (see p.141) specially for the job. Choose New Smart Playlist from the File menu and pick your rules. You might choose, for example, to exclude genres

Moving music from iPhone to computer

Purchased music

If you plug your iPhone into a computer other than the one it's paired with, it will allow you to copy any songs downloaded from the iTunes Store onto the computer. This option may pop up automatically; alternatively, click Transfer Purchases from… in the File menu whenever an iPhone is connected.

Of course, the music will only play back if the computer in question is one of the five machines authorized by your iTunes Store account (see p.120).

Other music

As with iPods, you can't copy music *not* purchased at the iTunes Store from iPhone to computer. This setup is designed to stop people sharing copy-righted music, but can be a real pain if your computer is stolen or destroyed, and the only version of your music collection you have left is the one stored on your iPhone.

In the last few years, several third-party applications have appeared that allow you get around the rules with regard to the iPod. These have never been for-mally recognized by Apple, but they've generally worked well. If past experi-ence is anything to go by, it will only be a matter of time before similar software appears for

the iPhone. The most likely suspects in the race to publish such tools are The Little App Factory, who currently make iPodRip (pictured), and Kennett Net, who produce Music Rescue:

The Little App Factory thelittleappfactory.com
Kennett Net kennettnet.co.uk

Smart Playlist			

☑ Match [all ⬍] of the following rules:

Genre ⬍	is ⬍	Electronica	⊖ ⊕
Bit Rate ⬍	is less than ⬍	320	kbps ⊖ ⊕
Date Added ⬍	is in the last ⬍	6	months ⬍ ⊖ ⊕

☑ Limit to [3] [GB ⬍] selected by [random ⬍]
☐ Match only checked items
☑ Live updating

(Cancel) (OK)

such as spoken word, or tracks over a certain length. Or you might limit the playlist to songs recently added to iTunes.

Once you're happy with your rules, pick a size using the Limit check box. For example, if you have an 8 gigabyte iPhone you might choose to dedicate 3 or 4 gigabytes to music. By checking the Live updating box, you'll ensure that the contents of the playlist change automatically as tracks meet or fail to meet the criteria you've specified. Finally, connect the iPhone, select its icon and, under the Music tab, set iTunes to sync your new playlist with the iPhone.

If you need to go back and change any of your rules at any time, highlight the playlist in the Source list and choose Edit Smart Playlist from the iTunes File menu.

> **TIP:** If you're a Mac user, you could also specify that you only want your iPhone to include music with album artwork – in order to make best use of the Cover Flow feature. To achieve this, download and install the free Tracks Without Artwork To Playlist script from dougscripts.com. Then set your iPhone Smart Playlist to ignore all tracks in the "no-artwork playlist" that the script generates.

Adding music from other computers

By default, if you plug your iPhone into any computer other than the one it's currently paired with, iTunes won't let you copy music onto the phone without blanking what's already on there. There's no harm in doing this – you can always sync with the original computer later – but it does mean that you can't easily stock up an iPhone from more than one computer.

This setup is designed to prevent the unauthorized copying of music. However, it's a real pain if you have more than one computer, or if you want to copy something copyright-free from a friend's Mac or PC.

The way around this limitation is to transfer the actual song files from one computer to the other. It probably goes without saying that sharing copyrighted music in this way is against the law. But it's fine for non-copyrighted music, or for moving music between your two computers, for example. Here's how it works:

▶ First, locate the files you want to copy. This can be done by browsing your iTunes music folder (see p.134), or by selecting an item in iTunes, clicking the File menu and choosing Show in Finder or Show in Windows Explorer.

▶ Next, copy those files or folders onto a portable hard drive, key drive or data disc. (Annoyingly, unlike with an iPod, you can't enable an iPhone as a hard drive and use it to copy the files across.)

▶ Drag the files onto the target computer and import them into iTunes in the usual way (see p.125).

Playing music on the iPhone

Once your iPhone is loaded up with tunes, you're ready to adjust its on-board audio settings (see box on p.152) and start listening.

Browsing lists

Tap iPod on the Home screen and the buttons will appear along the bottom to let you browse Playlists, Artists or Songs. Each button brings up a list and – as usual – you can either browse by flicking or jump to a specific letter by dragging your finger down the alphabetical list on the right.

Editing the options

The More button reveals further options for browsing. Depending on your listening habits, these might be more useful than the default options. For instance, classical buffs will want instant access to Composers, while radio lovers will want to front-load Podcasts.

Drop your browse option of choice over the one you least rarely use

To replace an existing browse icon with a different one, click More, then Edit, and then simply drag the new icon onto the old one.

You can also drag the icons at the bottom into any order.

147

Now playing…

When you are actually listening to your chosen cut, the iPhone offers a host of options and displays any available artwork for the track you have selected. Most of the controls are pretty intuitive and need little elaboration, but for those of you who have just landed from Mars, here's a run-through of what's on offer.

▶ **Pause/Play a song** Tap ❙❙ and ▶ respectively, or press the mic button on the iPhone headset.

▶ **To skip** to the start of the current or next song, tap ❙◀◀ or ▶▶❙. In a podcast or audiobooks these buttons skip between chapters. You can also skip forward by quickly pressing the mic button on the iPhone headset twice.

▶ **To rewind or fast forward** within the song you are listening to, press and hold ❙◀◀ or ▶▶❙.

An alternative way to rewind or fast-forward is to tap the album artwork of the current track to view a "scrubber" and navigate visually

▶ **To see the track list** of all the songs of the current album, tap the 🔲 button. Tap again to get back to the now-playing screen.

> **TIP:** To rate the current track, double-tap the album cover or hit 🔲. Then drag your finger across the five dots near the top of the screen. Your ratings are copied back to iTunes next time you sync, where they can be used in Smart Playlists or to remind you to junk poorly rated tunes.

> **TIP:** You can have your iPhone play music, podcasts or videos for a certain amount of time and then switch off – like the sleep function of an alarm clock. Tap Clock and then Timer, and choose a number of minutes or hours. Then tap When Time Ends, choose Sleep iPod, and hit Start.

Cover Flow

A few years ago, Cover Flow was a stand-alone application, created by independent programmer Jonathan del Strother, that iTunes users could download as an alternative way to browse their music libraries. Apple liked it so much they bought the technology and incorporated it into iTunes, and then the iPhone.

Cover Flow is a slick-looking graphical interface for "flicking through" your music's album artwork, so it's perfectly suited to the iPhone, where you really *can* flick. It's like rooting around the record bins of your favourite music store. To switch to the Cover Flow view on the iPhone, simply rotate the device through ninety degrees. The built-in accelerometer recognizes the shift of axis and displays your music library by its artwork. To view the track listing of an album, either tap the relevant image or hit ❶. Then tap any of the songs in the list to set it playing.

The only disadvantage of Cover Flow mode is that you don't have access to Shuffle, Repeat or Ratings.

▶ **To adjust the volume** drag the onscreen slider to the left and right, or use the physical buttons on the left side of the iPhone.

▶ **To go "up" a level** tap ← or swipe to the right over the album artwork image. Whilst browsing, you can return to the Now Playing screen at any time using the [Now Playing] button – a big improvement on the way it works on an iPod.

Shuffle and Repeat

The controls for Repeat and Shuffle (random selection) can be accessed by tapping the artwork of the current track:

▶ **To repeat all songs in the list** tap the ⟲ icon until it appears highlighted in sky blue.

▶ **To repeat only the current track** tap ⟲ until the icon displays a small circle containing a 1.

▶ **To turn off Repeat** tap the ⟲ until it appears whited out.

▶ **To turn Shuffle on or off** for the current songs in the list, tap ⤬.

> TIP: Whilst browsing your music collection, any list of songs will include a Shuffle option at the top. Click to start a random selection of the current list.

Deleting music from an iPhone

As with the iPods, you can't delete unwanted music directly from an iPhone. Instead, simply delete the track in iTunes and it will be deleted from your iPhone next time you connect. Or...

▶ **If you want the music on iTunes but not on your iPhone**, uncheck the little boxes next to the names of the offending tracks, and in the iPhone syncing options, choose "Only update checked songs".

▶ **If you don't want to uncheck the songs,** since this will stop them playing in iTunes too, sync your iPhone with a specific playlist (see p.143) and remove the offending songs from that playlist.

On-the-go playlists

The iPhone lets you create playlists on the fly when you are out and about, and then sync them back into iTunes next time you connect to your computer.

To create a new playlist, tap Playlists and choose On-The-Go. The iPhone will show you a list of all your songs, which you can add to by tapping. Less obviously, you can also click any of the buttons at the bottom of the screen to browse by album, playlist, artist and so on, and add tracks from there. When you are finished compiling, tap Done.

You can return to and change your new playlist at any time. Tap Playlists, then On-The-Go, and hit Edit. Next:

▶ **To add further tracks** tap +.

▶ **To move a song higher or lower in the list** drag the three horizontal bars next to the song.

Burning CDs & DVDs

If you'd like to share a playlist that you've created on your iPhone, simply highlight the relevant list in iTunes, check the bottom of the window to make sure the playlist isn't too long to fit on a CD (most discs take up to 70 or 80 minutes), insert a blank CD and press the Burn Disc button. In addition to regular audio CDs, you can also create data CDs/DVDs, which store up to 12–50 hours of music but can only be read by computers rather than hi-fis. To create a data CD, open the Burning pane of the Advanced section of iTunes Preferences (see p.45).

▶ **To delete a song** tap ⊖ and then the Delete button. (Fear not, this will only delete the track from the list, not the iPhone itself.)

▶ **To start again** tap Clear Playlist.

Music settings

The iPhone offers various options for audio playback. You'll find these by clicking Settings on the Home screen and then scrolling down to iPod.

▶ **Sound Check** This feature enables the iPhone to play all tracks at a similar volume level so that none sound either too quiet or too loud. Because these automatic volume adjustments are pulled across from iTunes, the Sound Check feature also has to be enabled within iTunes on your computer. To do this, launch iTunes and open Preferences (from the iTunes menu on a Mac and the Edit menu on a PC) then, under the Playback tab tick the Sound Check box.

▶ **EQ** Lets you assign an equalizer preset to suit your music and earphones. Note that you can also assign EQ settings to individual tracks in iTunes (see p.136).

▶ **Volume Limiter** Lets you put a cap on the volume level of the iPhone's audio playback (including audio from videos), to remove the risk that you might damage your ears or indeed your earphones. Tap Volume Limit and drag the slider to the left or right to adjust the maximum volume level. If you're a parent, you might also want to tap Lock Volume Limit and assign a combination code to prevent your kids from upping the volume level without your permission.

▶ **Audiobook Speed** Audiobooks recorded in certain file formats can be sped up or slowed down without making the reader sound like a bass-baritone or colaratura soprano. Tap here to choose from three speed options.

10 Video

How to download or roll your own

There's nothing particularly revolutionary about a phone or portable media player being able to handle video files. What's different about the iPhone is the size and clarity of its screen, the user-friendly controls and the decent battery life. The iPhone will play video for around six or seven hours before running out of juice – more than enough for a couple of average feature films.

Just as with music, before you can transfer videos or movies to your iPhone, you first have to get them into iTunes. This can be done in various ways: you can either download movies or TV shows from iTunes or import video from existing files or DVDs. It's even possible to record from television. Let's look at each option in turn…

Downloading videos from iTunes

Since the launch of the video iPod in October 2005, the iTunes Store has offered an ever-growing list of movies, TV shows and music videos. Downloading videos from the iTunes Store works in just the same way as with music. After you've downloaded a video file, it will be deposited in your iTunes Library. Depending on what sort of movie file it is, it will show up under one of three categories on the left side of the iTunes window – music videos appear in Music, feature films under Movies and television episodes under TV shows.

Once downloaded, it only takes a couple of clicks to transfer the video files to your iPhone (see p.162).

Video podcasts

In addition to pay-to-download video, iTunes offers access to scores of video podcasts. Ranging from the comedic (*The Ricky Gervais Podcast*) to the didactic (*Learn Excel with MrExcel*), video podcasts offer ideal journey-to-work-sized chunks of video, and they're free to boot. See p.164 for more information.

Importing existing video files

If you have video files on your computer and you want to get them onto your iPhone, you first need to convert them to a compatible format. In most cases (with MOV, MPEG and MP4 files) this is as simple as dragging the files into your iTunes library, highlighting them in the Song List and then selecting "Convert Selection for iPod" from the iTunes Advanced menu.

Once that's done, you can delete the older file from iTunes (check the Date Added column in the Song List to be sure which is which). Then you're ready to upload the videos to your phone in the normal way (see p.162).

With certain video files, however, you may find that this approach doesn't work. In these cases, you need to grab some extra software to help you convert the files to the necessary format:

▶ **QuickTime Pro** apple.com/quicktime/pro (PC and Mac)
QuickTime Pro, which costs $30/£20, is the advanced version of Apple's free media player and can handle most video file types (though not Windows Media). Once you have your video file open in QuickTime, simply press Export in the File menu and choose the "Movie to iPod" option. Take the resulting file and drag it onto the Movies icon in iTunes.

▶ **Video2Go** onlymac.de/indexe.html (Mac only)
This $10 application is even simpler than QuickTime Pro. It lets you browse for video files already on your Mac, then handles the conversion and drops the converted files straight into iTunes.

▶ **ffmpegX** homepage.mac.com/major4 (Mac only)

This unpronounceable tool (which is free to download and use but requests a $15 donation toward the cost of its development) gives complete control over various file format settings. However, to get it working you'll need to install a couple of other free files, and to mess about a bit with a few settings. For a clear tutorial, see: arstechnica.com/guides/tweaks/ipod-video.ars/3

> ▶ TIP: Mac owners can export iPod-ready versions of their home movies from iMovie HD via the Share option in the File menu. Click the QuickTime button and choose Expert Settings, then "Movie to iPod (320x240)".

Video formats

Video files are more confusing than most, as you have to worry not only about the file format (which you can usually tell by the file extension: eg .mov and .avi) but also the "codec" (compression technique) used to create the file. To make things even more complex, various other factors – such as frames per second and audio formats – may also affect whether a particular file can play back on a particular piece of hardware or software.

In short, the iPhone support files in the .m4v, .mp4 and .mov formats are created using H.264 and MPEG-4 codecs. In full, the supported video specifications are as follows:

▶ **H.264 video**, up to 1.5 Mbps, 640 by 480 pixels, 30 frames per second, Low-Complexity version of the H.264 Baseline Profile with AAC-LC audio up to 160 kbps, 48kHz, stereo audio in .m4v, .mp4 and .mov file formats.

▶ **H.264 video**, up to 768 kbps, 320 by 240 pixels, 30 frames per second, Baseline Profile up to Level 1.3 with AAC-LC audio up to 160 kbps, 48kHz, stereo audio in .m4v, .mp4 and .mov file formats.

▶ **MPEG-4 video**, up to 2.5 Mbps, 640 by 480 pixels, 30 frames per second, Simple Profile with AAC-LC audio up to 160 kbps, 48kHz, stereo audio in .m4v, .mp4 and .mov file formats.

Importing DVDs

In most cases, it's perfectly possible to get DVDs onto your iPhone. In some countries this may not be strictly legal when it comes to copyrighted movies, but as long as you're only importing your own DVDs for your own use, no one is likely to mind. The main problem is that it's a bit of a hassle. A DVD contains so much data that it can take more than an hour to "rip" each movie to your computer to a format that'll work with with iTunes and an iPhone. And if the disc contains copy protection (see box, below), then it's even more of a headache.

Using HandBrake

Of the various free tools available for getting DVDs into iTunes, ready for transfer to an iPhone, probably the best is HandBrake, which is available for both Mac and PC. Here's how the process works:

▶ **Download and install HandBrake** from handbrake.com.

▶ **Insert the DVD** and, if it starts to play automatically, quit your DVD player program.

DVD copy protection

DVDs are often encrypted, or copy protected, to stop people making copies or ripping the discs to their computers. PC owners can use a program such as AnyDVD (slysoft.com) to get around the protection, while Mac owners can turn to Fast DVD Copy (fastdvdcopy.com). This allows you to make a non-protected copy, which you can then get onto your phone in the standard way. For more on this process, and other applications that do the job, see *The Rough Guide to Macs & OS X*. Note that, in some countries, it may not be legal to copy an encrypted DVD.

▶ **Launch HandBrake** and it should detect the DVD (it may call it something unfriendly like "/dev/rdisk1"). Press Open, and wait until the application has scanned the DVD.

▶ **Plug in the three magic settings...**

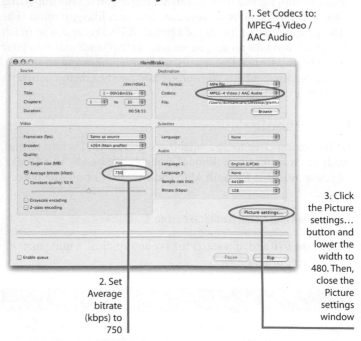

1. Set Codecs to: MPEG-4 Video / AAC Audio

3. Click the Picture settings... button and lower the width to 480. Then, close the Picture settings window

2. Set Average bitrate (kbps) to 750

▶ **Check the source** It's also worth taking a quick look at the "Title" dropdown menu within the Source section of HandBrake. If the list offers several options, choose the one that represents the largest amount of time (for example 01h22m46s) as this should be the main feature. If nothing of an appropriate length appears, then your DVD is copy protected (see box on previous page).

> **TIP:** If you check the "2-pass encoding" box, this will double the time it takes to process your movie, but the quality will be better, and with no increase in the size of the final file.

▶ **Subtitles** If it's a foreign-language film, set Dialogue and Subtitle options from the dropdown menus.

▶ **Rip** Hit the Rip button at the bottom of the window and the encoding will begin. Don't hold your breath.

▶ **Drop the file into iTunes** Unless you choose to save it somewhere else, the file will eventually appear on the Desktop. It will probably be in the region of a few hundred megabytes, depending on the length of the DVD. Drag the file onto the iTunes Library icon.

Other tools

There are various other DVD-ripping programmes out there. One good choice for PCs is ImTOO DVD-to-iPod Converter.

ImTOO imtoo.com/dvd-to-ipod-converter.html $29

For a few dollars more you could try out Xilisoft's DVD-to-iPod Suite, which guides you through the process in simple step-by-step style.

Xilisoft DVD to iPod Suite xilisoft.com

Recording from TV

If you want to create iPhone-friendly videos by recording from television, your best bet is to use a TV receiver for your computer. Some high-end PCs have these built in, but if yours doesn't you should be able to pick one up relatively inexpensively, and attach it to your PC or Mac via USB.

The obvious choice for Mac users is Elgato's superb EyeTV range of portable TV receivers, some of which are as small as a box of matches. You can either connect one to a proper TV aerial or, in areas of strong signal, just attach the tiny aerial that comes with the device.

With an EyeTV, it's easy to record TV shows and then export them directly into an iPhone-friendly format. For more info, see:

Elgato elgato.com

Hauppauge, Freecom and various other manufacturers produce similar products for PC owners. Browse Amazon or another major technology retailer to see what's on offer. If you can't find one that offers iPhone/iPod export functions, record the shows in any format of your choice and use QuickTime Pro to resave them for the iPhone.

> **TIP:** PC users can also export iTunes-friendly videos from certain TiVos. It's a bit of a hassle but can be useful. Search for TiVo online at engadget.com **for an excellent tutorial.**

Playing and managing videos

In iTunes

Videos downloaded from iTunes come correctly categorized as TV Shows, Music Videos or Movies. However, files you've imported from elsewhere will most likely arrive as Movies. To change this, select the relevant videos and choose Get Info from the File menu. Then, under the Video tab, choose the new category.

While you're there, you can also add or edit other info. In the case of TV shows, make sure that you add a title in the "Show" field; if this is left blank, iTunes will not display the file within the iPhone options pane under Video.

When a video is categorized as a Music Video it is lumped in with regular songs but retains a small Video icon in the Name column.

Any videos you import (rather than download from iTunes) will by default be classified as a "Movie" – even if it's actually a music video.

Click here to switch between list and thumbnail view.

Click the mini version of the video to view it in a separate window. For full screen mode use the View menu or press ⟦▪⟧ on the floating window's on-screen controls.

When you double-click a video it will start to play in the bottom-left panel. Click this thumbnail version to see the video in a separate window, or click the last of the five buttons on the bottom-left of the iTunes window to view the video in full-screen mode.

As before, click directly into a field in the Song List, or select one or more videos and press Apple+I (Mac) or Control+I (PC).

> TIP: Music videos can be added to regular music playlists in iTunes and on the iPhone. In iTunes, you can also combine TV shows and movies with songs in a playlist, but they won't appear when the playlist copies to the phone.

Video on the iPhone

Uploading

Connect your iPhone to your computer and click the Video tab in the Options pane. Here you can choose whether you want videos categorized as either Movies or TV Shows moved onto your phone and, if so, choose whether to sync all of them or just some. Video files can be huge, so being selective about it is generally a good idea.

To move any movies categorized as Music Videos over to your iPhone, the best thing to do is check the "Automatically update selective playlists only" option under the Music tab in the iPhone Options pane and check the iTunes "Music Videos" smart playlist (which automatically collects them together), making sure you also check the "Include music videos" box at the bottom. If this Smart Playlist gets too big, edit its rules (see p.141) to limit its size.

If iTunes won't let you copy a particular video file across, it could be in the wrong format. Select it in iTunes and choose "Convert Selection for iPod" from the iTunes Advanced menu.

Watching

On the iPhone, tap iPod and then Videos to find files categorized as either Movies or TV Shows (if the Videos button isn't visible, click More). Files categorized as Music Videos are listed under Playlists, Artists, etc, just like regular music files.

Tap the name of a video and it will start playing in landscape mode – you can't watch video files with the phone upright. When a video is playing, you can:

▶ **Pause** Tap once and then hit **II**. As usual, ▶ starts playing again.

▶ **Fast-forward and rewind** Tap once and drag the scrubber bar at the top of the screen. Alternatively, press and hold **I◀◀** or **▶▶I**.

▶ **Change format** To switch between widescreen and full-screen modes, double-tap anywhere or hit the ⌄⌃.

▶ **Stop watching** Hit "Done".

> TIP: A blue dot next to a TV Show in the Videos list on the iPhone means that the episode has not yet been viewed.

Deleting videos

Unlike with an iPod, you can delete Movie and TV Show video files (but not Music Videos) from your iPhone in order to free up space. The video files *won't* be deleted from iTunes next time you connect. To delete a video, swipe over its name in either direction, and press Delete.

Podcasts & radio

iPhone FM

The emergence of Internet radio in the 1990s was a great breakthrough, offering listeners countless stations, regardless of physical location. As this chapter shows, it's possible to get standard online radio shows onto an iPhone. However, it's a bit of a hassle and, in some cases, legally dodgy.

Hence the emergence of podcasts – audio and video shows aimed specifically at the MP3 generation. Podcasts are produced by everyone from the BBC to wannabe pundits operating out of their bedrooms. They're easy to make, they're even easier to find and download, and for the most part they're free.

Podcasts

Unlike most online radio, which is "streamed" across the Net in real time, podcasts are made available as files (usually MP3s) that can be downloaded and transferred to your iPhone or other digital music player. Podcasts are usually free and often consist of spoken content – current affairs, poetry, cookery, etc. There are many musical podcasts, too, though there's a grey area surrounding the distribution of copyrighted music in this way.

> TIP: If you want to stop your kids accessing podcasts through iTunes, check the relevant option under the Parental tab of iTunes Preferences.

The best way to understand podcasts is to think of them as "audio blogs". Like regular blogs, they are generally made up of a series of short episodes, or posts; you can subscribe to them via RSS (see below and p.176); and they are nearly all free.

Subscribing to podcasts

It's often possible to download a single podcast "show" directly from the website (look for an orange version of the logo pictured opposite) of whoever produced it, but it's far easier to use iTunes

RSS

RSS (Really Simple Syndication) is the technology used to allow people to "subscribe" to websites, blogs and podcasts. When you subscribe to a podcast, iTunes hooks up with an RSS file, or feed, which is stored online. This file contains information about all the episodes of the podcast and points iTunes to the relevant sound files. The RSS feed is written in a relatively simple code called XML (it's a bit like the HTML used to create webpages), which makes it quite easy to do yourself (see p.167).

to subscribe to each of the podcasts you're interested in. That way you have fresh news stories, debates, poems, music or whatever each day – ideal for the morning journey to work.

Open iTunes and click Podcasts in the Source List. Next, click the Podcast Directory link and browse or search for interesting-looking podcasts. When you find one that looks up your street, click subscribe and iTunes will automatically download the most recent episode to your iTunes Library, ready for transfer to your iPhone. (Depending on the podcast, you may also be offered all the previous episodes to download.)

To change how iTunes handles podcasts, look under the relevant tab in iTunes Preferences. For example, if disk space is at a premium on your system, tell iTunes to delete older episodes after a week or so.

On the iPhone...

To upload your podcasts onto your iPhone, connect the phone to the computer and click the Podcasts tab. You can choose to upload all your podcasts or be selective. Browsing and playing podcasts works the same as with music, with one difference: in the case of video podcasts, you can delete them directly from the iPhone to free up space. This can only be done, however, if you access the podcast via the Videos button, rather than the Playlists button.

Creating your own podcast

Once you've subscribed and listened to a few podcasts you might decide it's time to turn your hand to broadcasting and get in on the action. Without going into too much detail, this is how it's done via the iTunes Music Store:

▶ **Record your episode** This can be done pretty easily using a microphone and any of the programs we mention on p.127. When you're finished, save the episode in MP3 or AAC format.

▶ **Create an RSS feed** This is a bit fiddly, but you'll soon get the hang of it. You need nothing more than a text editor, which you'll already have in the form of Notepad (PC) or TextEdit (Mac). For full details on writing your RSS file, read the Apple tutorial and sample file at apple.com/itunes/podcasts/techspecs.html

▶ **Upload your podcast** Find or hire some Web space (most Internet connection accounts offer a bit for free), and use an FTP program to upload both the RSS feed and your audio files.

▶ **Test your feed** Make sure you're connected to the Internet and then open iTunes. Choose Subscribe to Podcast... from the Advanced menu and enter the URL (online address) of your RSS feed file. If your podcast automatically downloads into iTunes, you know that everything is working fine.

▶ **Submit your podcast to iTunes** From iTunes click the Music Store link in the Source List, then find your way to the store's Podcasts page and click the big "Submit a Podcast" button. Once you've entered the URL of your feed and a few other details, just sit back and wait for an email from Apple telling you that your podcast has been accepted.

Submit a Podcast

Radio

Podcasts are perfectly suited to the iPhone, but occasionally you may long for radio shows that aren't available in this form. After all, there are scores of stations streamed across the Internet. iTunes includes direct access to many (if you can't see the Radio icon on the left of the window, open Preferences and check the Radio box) and you'll find countless more at a directory such as:

About Radio radio.about.com

The problem is that most of the content from these stations isn't available to the iPhone – which can't currently run Real Player or Windows Media Player, which most online stations use to broadcast online. However, there are programs available for getting around this by recording online radio shows in real time and saving them onto your hard drive as MP3 files, ready to be imported into iTunes and transferred to your iPhone. Two popular examples are RadioLover and HiDownload:

HiDownload hidownload.com (PC)
RadioLover bitcartel.com/radiolover (Mac)

Be aware, however, that depending on your country, the station, and what you do with the download, recording from a radio stream may not be strictly legal.

> **TIP:** Two other ways to get radio on your iPhone are to buy earphones with a built-in FM receiver and to record from a regular FM radio onto your Mac or PC (see p.126).

Internet

12 The Web

Safari and beyond

The iPhone certainly isn't the first mobile device to offer Web browsing. But arguably it's the first one to provide tools that make it a pleasure as opposed to a headache. As discussed earlier, the iPhone comes with a nearly fully fledged version of the Safari Web browser. It can't do everything – Flash and Java items won't display, at the time of writing – but it's still one of the most impressive mobile Web devices to have ever been produced.

The basics

Make sure you have a phone signal (or even better a Wi-Fi signal), as discussed in the Connecting chapter, and tap Safari on the Home screen. Then…

▶ **Enter an address** Click at the top of the screen, tap ⊗ to clear the current address and start typing. Note the ".com" key for quickly completing addresses.

▶ **Search Google** Click at the top of the screen, tap in the Google field and start typing. When you're finished, hit Google. If you want to switch from Google to Yahoo! searching, look within Settings > Safari > Search Engine. Of course, you can also visit any search engine manually and use it in the normal way. For more search tips, see p.178.

> TIP: You can see the full URL of any link by tapping and holding the relevant text or image. (This is equivalent to hovering over a link with a mouse and looking at the status bar at the bottom of a normal Web browser.)

▶ **To follow a link** Tap once. If you did it by accident, press ✖.

▶ **Reload/refresh** If a page hasn't loaded properly, or you want to make sure you're viewing the latest version of the page, click ↻.

▶ **Send an address to a friend** When viewing a page, click at the top of the screen and tap Share. A new email will appear with the link in the body and the webpage's title in the subject line.

▶ **Zoom** Double-tap on any part of a page – a column, headline or picture, say – to zoom in on it or zoom back out. Alternatively,

History & cache

Like most browsers, Safari on the iPhone stores a list of each website you visit. These allow the iPhone to offer suggestions when you're typing an address but can also be browsed – useful if you need to find a site for the second time but can't remember its address. To browse your history, look at the top of your Bookmarks list, accessible at any time via the ꮯ icon. To clear your history, look for the option in Settings > Safari.

Unfortunately, despite storing your history, Safari doesn't "cache" (temporarily save) each page you visit in any useful way. This is a shame, as it means you can't quickly visit a bunch of pages for browsing when you've got no mobile or Wi-Fi reception. It also explains why using the Back button is slower on the iPhone than on a computer – when you click ◀, you download the page in question afresh rather than returning to a cached version.

"pinch out" with your finger and thumb (or any two digits of your choice). Once zoomed, you can drag the page around with one finger.

Multiple pages

Just like a browser on a Mac or PC, Safari on the iPhone can handle multiple pages at once. These are especially useful when you're struggling with a slow connection, and you don't want to close a page that you may want to come back to later. The only pain is that you can't tap a link and ask it to open in a new window.

▶ **Open a new page** Tap ⬚, then New Page.

▶ **Switch between pages** Tap ⬚ and flick left or right. To close a page, tap ⊗.

Opening links in new windows

The multiple webpages function is great. Annoyingly, however, the iPhone doesn't currently offer any way to open a link on the current page in a new window. To get around this, grab Richard Herrera's clever little bookmarklet, which allows you to make all links on any page open in a new window simply by clicking a special bookmark entry. To find the link, search iPhone at:

DocTyper doctyper.com

Bookmarks

Bookmarks are always handy, but when using a device without a mouse and keyboard, they're even handier than usual.

The basics

To bookmark a page to return to later on the iPhone, click ✚. To retrieve a bookmark, tap 📖, browse and then click the relevant entry. It's also possible to edit your bookmarks list on the iPhone:

▶ **To delete a bookmark or folder** Tap Edit followed by the relevant ⊖ icon. Hit delete to confirm.

▶ **To edit a bookmark or folder** Tap Edit, then hit the relevant entry and type into the name and URL fields.

▶ **To move a bookmark or folder** Tap Edit and slide it up or down using the ≡ icon. Alternatively, tap Edit, then hit the relevant entry and use the third option down to pick the folder you'd like to move the bookmark or folder into.

Importing bookmarks from your Mac or PC

iTunes lets you quickly transfer bookmarks from a Mac or PC to your iPhone. Just connect your iPhone and click its icon in iTunes. Under the Info tab, check the relevant box under Web Browser. The bookmarks will move across to the iPhone, though they can be easy to miss: if you use Safari on your Mac or PC, you'll find them within two folders labelled Bookmarks Menu and Bookmarks Toolbar.

Likewise, bookmarks from the iPhone will appear back in your browser. In Safari, you won't find them in the Bookmarks menu, however: you'll have to click Show All Bookmarks or the 📖 icon.

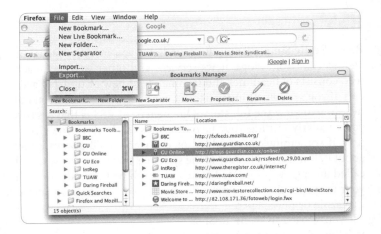

Importing Firefox bookmarks

At the time of writing, the iPhone only syncs bookmarks with Safari or Internet Explorer – not Firefox. However, it is perfectly possible to get your Firefox bookmarks onto your phone. Open Firefox, click the Bookmarks menu and choose "Organize Bookmarks…". When the Bookmarks Manager pops up, click the File menu, choose Export… and save the file on your desktop.

Next, open Safari or Internet Explorer, choose the Import option in the File menu, and point to the file you just created. Your Firefox bookmarks will then be pulled into IE or Safari, ready to be edited (if necessary) and copied to your iPhone.

> TIP: Though you can copy Firefox bookmarks onto the
> iPhone, you can't have iTunes update Firefox with
> bookmarks added on the phone. One work-around for
> this is to email yourself the URL each time you bookmark a page
> on the phone (see p.172) and add it to Firefox on your Mac or PC.

RSS

RSS – Really Simple Syndication – allows you to view "feeds" or "newsfeeds" from blogs, news services and other websites. Each feed consists of headlines and summaries of new or updated articles. If you see something you think you'd like to read, click on the headline to view the full story. One benefit of RSS is that it saves you regularly visiting your favourite sites to check for new content: if something's been added or changed, you'll always know about it. But the real beauty of the system is that you can use a tool called an aggregator or feed reader to combine the feeds from all your favourite sites. It's almost like having your own personalized magazine or newspaper.

If you're used to using RSS, you'll be disappointed by the current lack of RSS support on the iPhone. But fear not – you can still sign up with a Web-based aggregator and access your feeds via a customized webpage either on your phone or your computer. The main online aggregators include:

Bloglines bloglines.com/mobile
Google Reader reader.google.com/reader/m
My Yahoo! m.yahoo.com/start
Digg Reader digg.com/iphone#_stories

Just sign up with one of the above and add the feeds you're interested in. To do this, either use the search tools on the site or (when back on your Mac or PC) click the New Feed link and paste in feed addresses copied from your favourite sites.

Other browsing tips

Searching for text on a page

One very useful tool currently missing in the iPhone version of Safari is the ability to search for text within a page. This is especially annoying when you follow a link in Google and end up on a very long page with no idea where your search terms appear.

A workaround for this is to get into the habit, when searching the Web, of visiting Google's "cached" (saved and indexed) version of a webpage rather than the "live" version. You'll find a link for this option next to each of the results when you search Google. Click "Cached" and see a version of the target page that's got each of your search terms highlighted in a different colour throughout – almost as good as being able to click Find.

Rough Guides Travel
travel and music guide publishers; includes an online guide to destinations throughout the world,...
www.**roughguides**.com/ - 24 k - Cached - Similar pages

Webpage display problems

If a webpage looks weird on screen – bad spacing, images overlapping, etc – there are two likely causes. First, it could be that the page isn't properly "Web compliant". That is, it looked OK on the browser the designer tested it on (Internet Explorer, for example), but not on other browsers (such as Safari or Firefox). The solution is to try viewing the page through another browser.

Second, it could be that the page includes elements based on technologies that the iPhone doeesn't yet handle, such as Flash, Real and Windows Media. This is especially likely to be the problem if there's a gap in an otherwise normal page.

If a webpage looks OK, but different from the version you're used to seeing on your Mac or PC, it could be that the website in question has been set up to detect your browser and automatically offer you a small-screen version.

iPhone Googling Tips

Given that your connection speed may be low when out and about, and because you don't have access to Google Toolbar and the like, it makes sense to hone your search skills for use on the iPhone. All the following tricks work on a PC or Mac, too.

Basic searches

Googling this...	Find pages containing...
william lawes	the terms "william" and "lawes"
"william lawes"	the phrase "william lawes"
william OR lawes	either "william", "lawes" or both
william -lawes	"william" but not "lawes"

All these commands can be mixed and doubled up. Hence:

"william lawes" OR "will lawes" -composer	*either* version of the name but not the word "composer"

Synonyms

~mac	"mac" and related words, such as "Apple" and "macintosh"

Definitions

define:calabash	definitions from various sources for the word "calabash". You can also get definitions of a search term from answers.com by clicking the link in the right of the top blue strip on the results page.

Flexible phrases

"william * lawes" | "william john lawes" as well as just "william lawes"

Search within a specific site

site:bbc.co.uk "jimmy white" | pages containing Jimmy White's name within the BBC website. This is often far more effective than using a site's internal search.

Search Web addresses

"arms exports" inurl:gov | the phrase "arms exports" in the webpages with the term gov in the address (ie government websites)

Search page titles

train bristol intitle: timetable | pages with "timetable" in their titles, and "train" and "bristol" anywhere in the page

Number & price ranges

1972..1975 "snooker champions" | the term "snooker champions" and any number (or date) in the range 1972–1975

$15..$30 "snooker cue" | the term "snooker cue" and any price in the range $15–30

Search specific file types

filetype:pdf climate change statistics | would find pdf documents (likely to be more "serious" reports than webpages) containing the terms "climate", "change" and "statistics"

Viewing online PDFs and Word documents

The iPhone *can* view Word, Excel and PDF documents on the Web, but it can take quite a while for them to appear, as the iPhone has to download them and create an iPhone-friendly preview version before anything is displayed.

So… be patient. Or, if you can't be patient, and you're following a link from Google to a PDF, Word or Excel doc, click the "View As HTML" link instead of the main link to the document. This way you'll get a faster-loading text only version.

[PDF] **OFFICE OF THE UNITED NATIONS HIGH COMMISSIONER FOR HUMAN RIGHTS ...**
File Format: **PDF/Adobe Acrobat** - View as HTML
The international human rights treaties of the United Nations that establish committees of experts (often referred to as "treaty bodies") to monitor their ...
www.unhchr.ch/**pdf**/**report.pdf** - Similar pages

Webpages specially optimized for the iPhone

Though the iPhone can handle almost all webpages, some are specially designed to work perfectly on the iPhone screen – with no zooming required. See p.226 for a list of our favourites.

Safari options on the iPhone

Though you're unlikely to need them, you'll find various browsing preferences under Settings > Safari. Here you can empty your cache and history (useful if Safari keeps crashing, or you want to hide your tracks), and turn the following on or off:

▶ **Javascript**: a ubiquitous way to add extra functions to websites

▶ **Cookies**: files that websites save on your phone to allow customizations such as "we recommend"

▶ **Pop-up blocker**: stops pop-up pages (mainly ads) from opening

13 Email

How to set up and use Mail

Having email available wherever you are completely changes your relationship with it. It becomes more like text messaging – but much better. Like recent Macs, the iPhone comes with an email program known as Mail. However, the version on the iPhone has been cut down to its bare bones.

Setting up email accounts

Setting up AOL, Gmail, Hotmail and Yahoo!

The iPhone comes preconfigured to work with email accounts from AOL, Gmail, Hotmail and Yahoo!. If you use one of these email providers, you may be used to logging in via a website (and indeed, it's perfectly possible to do this on the iPhone). However, it's much faster and more convenient to use a proper mail program such as Mail on the iPhone.

To set up one of these accounts, just tap Mail, choose your account provider from the list and enter your normal log-in details. You may be prompted to log in to your account on the Web and enable POP3 access (see box, overleaf). You can do this via Safari on your iPhone, or using a computer.

Setting up other email accounts

If you have an email account that you use with Mail, Outlook or Outlook Express, then it's simple to copy across your account details onto your iPhone. This won't copy across the actual messages – just the details about your accounts so that you can begin

Email jargon buster

Email can be collected and sent in various ways, the most common being POP, IMAP and Exchange – all of which are supported by the iPhone. If you're using an account from your ISP, you may find you can choose between IMAP and POP. Here's the lowdown on each type:

▶ **POP** (or **POP3**) email accounts can be sent and received via an email program such as Mail or Outlook. Each time you check your mail, new messages are downloaded from your provider's mail server onto your computer or phone. It's a bit like a real-world postal service – and, indeed, POP stands for Post Office Protocol. When using a computer, messages are usually deleted from the server as you download them, but it is possible to leave copies on the server so you can download them from other computers. By default, the iPhone doesn't delete the messages as it downloads them.

▶ **IMAP** An IMAP account can also be sent and received via an email program, but all the messages are based on your mail provider's server, not on your phone or computer. When you open your mail program, it downloads the email headers (from, to, subject, etc). Clicking on a message will download the body, but not delete it from the server. This can be a bit slow at times, but it means your archive – complete with mail folders – will be available at all times. It also means the amount of mail you can store will be limited by the server space offered by your provider. IMAP stands for Internet Message Access Protocol.

▶ **Exchange** Exchange is Microsoft's corporate system designed for corporations. If you use Outlook at work, it's likely that you're using an Exchange email account. iPhone can handle Exchange accounts, but only if IMAP access is enabled on the account. Ask your network administrator if this is possible.

▶ **Web access** Most POP, IMAP and Exchange email providers also let you send and receive email via a website. You can access your mail this way on the iPhone via Safari, though it's much more convenient to use Mail.

sending and receiving on the phone. To get things going, connect your iPhone to your Mac or PC, select its icon in iTunes and choose the Info tab in the main panel. Scroll down and check the boxes for each email account you want to copy across, and press Apply Now.

If you have an email account that you only access via the Web, rather than with an email program, and it isn't provided by AOL, Gmail, Hotmail or Yahoo!, then contact your provider to ask whether the account offers POP access. If it does, get the details and set up the account on the iPhone manually, as described below. If not, you could access the account on the Web via Safari, but you might prefer to get another account – Yahoo! is our top recommendation, since it supports Push email (see p.184).

Setting up an email account manually

If, for whatever reason, iTunes isn't able to copy across your email accounts, then you can set up your account manually. The iPhone supports all the most common email formats, including POP,

IMAP and Exchange (see box on p.182). You just need to get the relevant details from your provider or network administrator (or try to guess them) and plug them into the phone:

▶ Tap Settings > Mail > Add Account… > Other

▶ Choose from IMAP, POP or Exchange and ignore the other two. If you're not sure which to pick, try POP.

▶ Fill in the details. If, say, your email address was currently joebloggs@myisp.com, your username will probably be joebloggs (or possibly your full email address), your incoming mail server may be mail.myisp.com or pop.myisp.com; and your outgoing server may be smtp.myisp.com. Press Save when you're done.

Push mail versus normal mail

Traditionally, a computer or phone only receives new emails when its mail application contacts the relevant server and checks for new messages. On a computer, this happens automatically every few minutes – and whenever you click the Check Mail or Send/Receive button. On the iPhone, it only happens when you click Mail, unless you set up Auto-Check, as described on p.186.

By contrast, email accounts that support the "Push" system feed messages to the iPhone the moment they arrive on the server – which is usually just seconds after your correspondent clicks the send button. At the time of writing, Yahoo! is the only mainstream email provider offering Push mail compatible with the iPhone. Accounts are free and offer unlimited storage. To sign up for an account, visit:

Yahoo! mail.yahoo.com

If you want the convenience of push email without switching accounts, then one option is to set your existing account to forward all your mail to a free Yahoo! account, and set up both on the iPhone. The Yahoo account will alert you to new messages instantaneously, which will then appear in your regular account when you open Mail, allowing you to reply as normal. Ask your email provider whether they can activate forwarding for you.

Sending and receiving email

Using email on the iPhone works just as you'd expect. Tap Mail on the Home screen, and then…

▶ **Compose a message** Tap ✉. (If you have more than one account set up, first select the account you want to use from the list.) Alternatively, you can kick-start a message by tapping a name in Contacts, Recent or SMS and then tapping the contact's email address.

▶ **Reply or forward** Open a message, tap ↩ and choose the relevant option.

▶ **Delete a message** You can delete messages in the list view by swiping left or right and tapping Delete. However, it's usually quicker and more convenient to open the message and press 🗑. This way, you then jump to the next message.

> TIP: As with Safari, you can tap and hold a link in an email to reveal the full destination address. Useful for links in emails that seem a bit dodgy.

▶ **Zoom in and out** Double-tap and "pinch" respectively – just like with Safari. If you often find that you have to zoom in to read the text, try raising the minimum text size under Settings > Mail.

▶ **To attach a photo** You can't add an attachment to a message that you have already started, but you can tap Photos, select an image, and tap 🖼. Next tap Email Photo and type an accompanying message in the normal way. The email will be sent from the default account, which you can select under Settings > Mail.

▶ **Empty the Trash** From your Mail Accounts page, select an account and then tap the Trash icon to view deleted items. You can then permanently delete individual items by tapping Edit at the top and then the ⊖ button next to the offending item, hitting Delete to confirm. You can also tap Settings > Mail, choose an account, and then tap Advanced > Remove and choose to have messages in the Trash automatically deleted either never, or after a day, a week, or a month.

Tweaking the settings

Once your email account is up and running on your phone, scan through the Settings options to see what suits you. Some things to consider:

▶ **Message preview** If you'd like to be able to see more of each message without clicking it, press Settings > Email > Preview and increase the number of lines.

▶ **Auto-check** By default, your phone will only check for new messages when you open Mail or, if you're already using Mail, click ↻. If you'd like your phone to check your mail automatically, tap Settings > Email > Auto-Check and choose a time. Annoyingly, you can't have the phone check your email more regularly than every 15 minutes (presumably because Apple are keen to minimize network access). Yahoo! email users don't need to worry about this, as their account features Push Email (see box).

▶ **To/Cc** If you'd like to be able to see at a glance whether you were included in the To: or Cc: field of an email, tap Settings > Mail > Show To/Cc Label. A small icon will appear by each message preview stating "to" or "cc".

▶ **Sent mail** With a standard email account, messages sent from your iPhone won't get transferred to the Sent folder on your Mac or PC. If this bothers you, as you'd like to have a complete archive of your mail on your computer, turn on Always CC Myself under Settings > Mail. The downside is that every message you send will pop up in your iPhone inbox a few minutes later. The upside is that you'll get a copy of your sent messages next time you check your mail on your Mac and PC. You can copy these into your Sent folder manually, or set up a rule or filter to do it automatically.

▶ **Default account** If you have more than one email account set up on the iPhone, you can choose one to be the default account. This will be used whenever you create messages from other applications – such as when you email a picture from within Photos (see p.197). So choose the account that you're most likely to use in this way, which might not necessarily be the one you use the most.

▶ **Adding a signature** Even if you have a sign-off signature (name, contact details, etc) set up at home, it won't show up automatically when you use the same account from the iPhone. To set up a mail signature for your iPhone, tap Settings > Mail > Signature and then enter your signature.

Email problems

You can receive but not send

If you're using an account from your Internet Service Provider, you might find that you can receive emails on the iPhone but not send them. If you entered the details manually on the iPhone, go back and check that you inputted the outgoing mail server details correctly, and that your login details are right.

If that doesn't work, contact your ISP and ask them if they have an outgoing server address that can be accessed from anywhere, or if they can recommend a "port" for mobile access. If they can, add this number, after a colon, onto the name of your outgoing mail server – which you'll find by tapping Settings > Mail and choosing your account.

For example, if your server is smtp.myisp.com and the port number is 138, enter smtp.att.yahoo.com:138

There are messages missing

The most likely answer is that you downloaded them to your Mac or PC before your iPhone had a chance to do so. Most email programs are set up to delete messages from the server once they've successfully downloaded them. However, it's easy to change this.

First, open your mail program and view the account setting. If you use Apple Mail, click Mail > Preferences > Accounts. In most other programs, look under the Tools menu. Click the relevant account and look for a "delete from server" option, which is usually buried under Advanced.

Choose to have your program delete the messages one week after downloading them. This way your iPhone will have time to download each message before they get deleted. It also means you'll have access to more of your messages when checking your mail via the Web.

Messages don't arrive unless I check for them

Unless you use Yahoo! or another push mail system (see p.184), this is the default setting. If you'd rather have your iPhone check for mail automatically, switch the Auto-Check feature on and choose how frequently you want the iPhone to check. Look within Settings > Mail > Auto-Check. Of course, your phone will need to have either carrier or Wi-Fi reception to check-in with your account.

I get a copy of all the messages I send

It could be that Always CC Myself is switched on under Settings > Mail. But if you're using Gmail the most likely cause is that you have Use Recent Mode switched on. To turn this off, tap Settings > Mail and select your Gmail account; tap Advanced and you'll see the relevant slider at the bottom.

Extras

14 Photos

Pictures in your pocket

The iPhone serves both as a camera in itself and as a photo album to show off your digital photo collection – including pics taken with other cameras. This chapter offers some tips on using the iPhone's built-in camera before explaining how to get your existing images onto your phone.

The iPhone camera

The iPhone has a built-in two-megapixel digital camera. The bad news is, it has a fixed lens, no optical zoom, no white balance or scene-setting modes, no video capability, and produces pretty disappointing colours. However, you do get to frame your images using the whole screen.

To take a picture, simply tap the Camera button on the Home screen, aim and tap 📷. The results will hardly be professional, but they can be decent enough to capture a moment. Here are a few things you can try to get the most from the iPhone camera:

▶ **Hold it steady** The iPhone takes *much* better pictures when it's held steady, and when the subject of the picture is not moving. Try leaning on a wall, or putting both elbows on a table with the iPhone in both hands, to limit wobble.

▶ **Take photos outdoors** The iPhone takes much better images outside, in daylight, than it does inside or at night. However, too much direct light and the contrast levels hit the extremes.

▶ **White light** If you do take shots inside, expect to get better results in light that tends towards white, as opposed to that produced by more yellow bulbs.

The iPhone microscope

If you want to get up really close-in on your subject, consider combining your iPhone's camera with a magnifying lens or microscope. You can then go and make some new friends in this Flickr group:

Flickr group flickr.com/groups/424440@N23

▶ **Get close** To take a decent portrait, you'll need to be within a couple of feet of the subject's face. This way more pixels are devoted to face rather than background; in addition, the exposure settings are more likely to be correct.

▶ **Light source** Make sure that the light source is behind the camera and not behind the subject of the photograph.

The images you take are saved in the so-called Camera Roll, which can be found by tapping ▢ (when using the camera) or by looking within Photos. The images can be viewed and used in all the normal ways (see p.197).

Photographing contacts

One thing you can do with the camera is shoot pictures of friends and family and then assign them to relevant entries in the Contacts lists. Annoyingly, though, you have to create a contact entry first (see p.87) and add the image there; you can't create a new contact directly from a picture.

Removing the camera

In the US, several government and military organizations, and even a few commercial businesses, refuse to let employees bring camera phones onto their premises due supposed espionage risks. If that applies in your work place, you could have the camera removed. A company called iResQ will do the job for $100, including overnight shipping in both directions.

iResQ iresq.com/iphone

Putting existing pics on an iPhone

The iPhone can be loaded up with images from your computer. iTunes moves them across, in the process creating copies that are optimized for the phone's screen, thereby minimizing the disk space they occupy. iTunes can move images from an individual folder or from one of three supported photo-management tools:

▶ **iPhoto (Mac)** apple.com/iphoto
Part of the Apple's iLife package, which is free with all new Macs (and available separately for $79). Version 4.0.3 or later will sync with an iPhone, but version 6 is far superior.

▶ **Photoshop Album (PC)** adobe.com/photoshopalbum
Only version 2.0 or later will work; the application will cost you around $50/£40.

▶ **Photoshop Elements (PC)** adobe.com/photoshopelements
Like the above, but with far more editing tools and a $90/£60 price tag. You'll need version 3.0 or later.

These applications offer editing tools for colour balance and so on, and allow you to arrange your images into "albums", which will show up in a list on your iPhone. If you prefer, though, you

How to stop iPhoto popping up

If you sync your iPhone with iPhoto, when you connect the phone to your Mac, iPhoto may automatically launch and offer to import recent snaps taken with your camera phone. (If your Camera Roll is empty, this won't happen.) The way around this is to turn off syncing for photos. This won't delete any pics already on your phone. Then, whenever you want to transfer images between the phone and computer, temporarily switch syncing back on.

can keep your photos within a standard folder, such as the My Pictures folder in Windows, or the Pictures folder in OS X. Any subfolders within it will be treated as albums.

To copy across your photos, connect your iPhone to your computer and look under the Photos tab of the Options panel. Check the sync box then choose your application or folder. If your images are elsewhere use the Choose Folder option to browse for them. At the bottom of the window you will see a running total of how many pics you have selected to sync.

Viewing images on the iPhone

Once your images are on the phone, photo navigation is very straightforward. Tap Photos and choose an album – or tap Photo Library to see the images in all albums. Once you're viewing an individual image, you can:

▶**"Flick" left and right** to move to the previous or next photo.

▶ **Zoom in and out** Double-tap or "stretch" and "pinch" with two fingers.

▶ **Rotate the iPhone** to see the picture in landscape mode.

▶ **Hide or reveal the controls** Tap once anywhere on the image.

▶ **Email the photo**, assign it to a contact (so that it shows when they call), or set it as your wallpaper. Tap 📤.

As mentioned previously, one thing you *can't* currently do with a picture on the iPhone is send it via SMS.

Slideshows

To kickstart a slideshow, open an album and tap ▶. By default, the phone will show each photo for three seconds, but you can change this by tapping Settings > Photos > Slideshows. The same screen lets you add *Star Wars*-esque transitions between photos, and turn on Shuffle (random order) and Repeat (so that the slideshow plays around and around until you beg it to stop).

Unlike colour-screen iPods, the iPhone doesn't allow you to connect to a TV to play your slideshows on a bigger screen.

Beyond photos

The iPhone's image capability isn't limited to photographs, of course. You can import any image saved in a common image format. So you could, for example, export PowerPoint presentations as JPEGs and import them to your phone as a photo album to save you lugging a laptop around. (Obviously, this will work best if you stick to large font sizes in the document.) It's easy to do this manually, though iPresent It automates the process for Mac users:

iPresent It zapptek.com

More tools

From clocks to stocks...

Like most modern phones, the iPhone offers a small menagerie of extra tools such as alarms, calendars and notes. The difference is that on the iPhone such tools are easy to use, nicely designed and accessible with one tap from the Home screen. This compares with fiddly interfaces and baffling menus on most other phones (as typified by the Motorola Razr, which helpfully puts Alarm Clock under the ☰ menu, within Office Tools).

On the iPhone, the extra tools have been variously referred to by Apple as "applications" and "widgets". This chapter glances briefly at each, and offers a few online alternatives for when they fall short.

Calculator

Paying no small tribute to the classic designs of German functionalist Dieter Rams, the look of the iPhone's calculator widget can be traced back to a calculator that Braun (for whom Rams worked)

produced for Apple in the mid-1980s. The iPhone's calculator might look great, and it's fine for basic calculations, but it has no

scientific functions. So if you're struggling with a square root or a non-linear algorithm, tap Safari and proceed to MiniCalc:

MiniCalc iphav.com

Calendar

The Calendar tool, whose icon on the Home screen permanently shows the correct date, lets you easily organize events and appointments, complete with reminder alerts. You can view your schedule by month or day, or in a list, though unfortunately not by week.

To add a new event, tap + (top-right), enter whatever data you like, and tap Save. To edit or delete an existing event, tap the relevant entry and use the Edit button or Trash icon.

iPhone calendars can be synchronized with your computer, but only if you use iCal or Entourage on a Mac, or Outlook on a PC. Once syncing is set up, calendar data is merged between your computer and phone, so deletions, additions or changes made in either place will be reflected in the other next time you sync.

> TIP: You can use Calendar instead of Notes to jot down thoughts on the move. Just add an event and use the Notes field. You can set a date and time when you think the jottings will be useful, and even set an alert. Both note and alarm will be copied back to your computer next time you sync.

Calendar alerts

You can set an alert to remind you of an impending event either as it happens or a certain numbers of minutes, hours or days beforehand. If you'd like to have these alerts presented visually, instead of via a sound, tap Settings > Sounds and turn off the Calendar Alert switch.

To sync your calendars, connect your iPhone to your computer, open iTunes, click the Info tab and check the boxes for moving either all or some of your calendars.

If your old phone has calendars on it that you want to use with your iPhone, first move them onto your computer and into iCal, Entourage or Outlook, just as you would with your old phone's address book (see p.78).

Annoyingly, if you use more than one calendar on your

One thing the iPhone Calendar tool doesn't currently support is to-do lists, such as those composed in iCal. Instead, you could try the free iPhone-optimized service at tadalist.com

Mac or PC (for Work, Home and Sport, say), they'll all look the same on the iPhone, and when you create a new event you can't choose which of your calendars you want to add it to. All you can do is specify one calendar to which all new events will be added. This is done within the sync options in iTunes.

Clock

To quickly check the time on your iPhone, look to the digital clock which is almost always present at the top of the screen. The Clock widget, meanwhile, offers four tools:

▶ **World Clock** Click **+** or Edit to add and remove locations. Cities where it's currently light will appear with a white clock-face; those where it's dark will appear in black. To order the list, click Edit and drag the ☰ icons. If you want to double-check that your phone has the correct time, tap Safari and visit:

OnlineClock.net onlineclock.net

▶ **Alarm** Use the **+** button to add as many alarms as you like. Each one can be customized with a label and alarm sound and set to repeat on certain days of the week. You can then turn individual alarms on or off in the list as you need them.

> TIP: If you're using the iPhone alarm, make sure you don't turn the phone onto Silent mode, or all you'll get is an on-screen message.

▶ **Stopwatch and Timer** As you'd expect, the Stopwatch counts up and the Timer counts down.

Maps

The Maps widget takes you into the world of Google Maps, where you can quickly find locations, get directions and even view satellite photos. You can zoom and scroll around the maps in the same way you would with webpages in Safari, double-tapping or "pinching" to zoom in and out. It works OK over EDGE, though it's far quicker through Wi-Fi.

 To get started, tap the Search box and type a city, town or region, place of interest, or a ZIP code or postcode. (As you type, the iPhone will try to predict the location based on previous map searches and address entries in your Contacts list.) You can also try to find a business in the area you are viewing by tapping the address field at the top and entering either the name of the business or something more general – such as "camera", "hotel", or "pizza". Note, however, that the results, which are pulled from Google Local, won't be anything like comprehensive.

> TIP: Your lists of bookmarked and recently viewed locations, and all addresses in your Contacts list, can be viewed at any time by tapping 📖.

Search results appear as a little red pin. Tap the ◉ button for further options such as adding the location as a bookmark or contact address, or getting the directions to or from that location...

Directions

The Maps tool provides driving directions from one place to another. To search for directions, tap 🔳 and enter start and end locations, either by entering search terms or tapping 📖 to browse for known and recent addresses. When you are ready, tap Route.

Once a journey is displaying, you can go through it one step at a time by tapping Start and using the arrow buttons to jump forward and back one stage. Alternatively, tap List to view all the stages as a series of text instructions. Tap any entry in the list to see a map of that part of the journey.

> TIP: For your return journey, reverse the directions given by your iPhone by tapping the ↺ button. If you can't see a ↺ button, tap List, then Edit.

Traffic conditions

In areas where the service is available, you can check the traffic conditions for your journey by tapping 🚗. The approximate driving time at the top of the iPhone screen will change to take account of the expected traffic and the roads will change colour:

▶ **Grey** No data currently available

▶ **Red** Traffic moving at less than 25 miles per hour

▶ **Yellow** Traffic moving at 25–50 miles per hour

▶ **Green** Traffic moving at more than 50 miles per hour

If you don't see any change in colour, you may need to zoom out a little. This action will also automatically refresh the traffic speed data.

More maps

Though Google Maps is probably the single best online map service, it may not always find what you're looking for. So bear in mind that you also have the Web at your fingertips, complete with scores of map sites, such as the following:

Multimap multimap.com
Transport For London tfl.gov.uk/maps
UrbanRail.net urbanrail.net
World Maps justmaps.org

Pictures as maps

One downside with any online map service is that they'll only work when you can get an Internet connection. For maps that you always want to be able to view – such as those for your local subway or tube system – you could instead store them as pictures. Simply drag maps from websites into your picture collection and iTunes will pull them across next time you sync. However, this will only work well with smallish maps; the text will be rendered illegible on larger ones, unless they're cut into smaller chunks.

The kind souls at iSubwayMaps have prepared and made available various maps in this format. They're free to download and convenient to use.

iSubwayMaps isubwaymaps.com

Notes

Notes is a simple application for jotting down thoughts on the go. Use the **+** button to bring up a new blank page and you're ready to type. When you're done, tap Done or use the envelope icon to email the note to yourself or others.

If you're hankering for something more fully featured (or which doesn't insist that you use the rather annoying Marker Felt font) you could try an online word processor accessed via Safari. Unfortunately, the excellent Google Docs (docs.google.com) won't currently work on the iPhone: you can log in and read but not type anything. Thankfully, there are alternatives, including gOffice – which has a great iPhone-friendly interface and lets you email your finished text as a Word document – and the easy-to-use iZoho, the iPhone version of Zoho Writer.

gOffice goffice.com
Zoho Writer izoho.com

Stocks

Another widget that relies on the Internet for its data, Stocks lets you view current values for any listed company. Well, not quite current – the prices are refreshed whenever you open the application, but are typically still about 20 minutes out of date.

Tap ❶ and then ✚ to add new companies to the list, or ➖ to delete one.

For more information about a specific company, tap ❷! to visit a Yahoo! screen with general search results as well as financial profiles and more. For more financial info, point Safari at:

BigCharts bigcharts.com

Weather

Pulling its data from Yahoo!, the Weather application does pretty much what you would expect. You can view current conditions along with a six-day forecast with temperature highs and lows, and graphics for sun, rain, snow and cloud.

Flicking the screen to the left or right lets you move between forecasts for different cities. To add new locations, tap **❼** followed by +. To delete locations, use the relevant ⊖ button. The number of dots at the bottom of the weather screen denotes how many cities are stored. Tapping the **Y!** button, bottom-left, takes you to city information provided by Yahoo!.

If the Weather widget doesn't provide enough information for you, try an iPhone-optimized weather website – many of which amassed on the horizon within weeks of the iPhone's launch. These range from ForeFlight, for pilots or aviation staff, to Weather iWidget, for satellite images.

iWeathr iweathr.com/iweathr
ForeFlight iphone.foreflight.com
MyMetar mymetar.com/iphone/index.jsp
Weather iWidget weather.iwidget.org

YouTube

The YouTube widget, which provides direct access to content from the world's most popular video-sharing website, was announced only days before the iPhone's launch. Why a separate widget for a specific website? The main reason is that the normal YouTube website won't currently work on an iPhone, as the website requires Flash. In addition, Apple were keen to promote their new-found relationship with YouTube, having struck a deal which sees videos from the site made available via the company's home media-player device, Apple TV.

At the time of writing, however, the iPhone still can't access all of the clips on the full website. Only those which YouTube have re-encoded in the correct format are available. Thankfully, that includes most of the best ones.

Since YouTube videos are streamed from the Internet in real time, a good Internet signal is essential. As such, this widget is a lot more fun via Wi-Fi than via EDGE.

Finding clips

Tap YouTube and you can either search for clips or browse by the following categories.

▶ **Featured** Staff recommendations from YouTube, typically an entertaining mix of band promos, animations and the absurd.

> TIP: To choose which buttons appear at the bottom of the YouTube list screen, tap More and then Edit, and then drag icons from the top to the bottom to overwrite the current selections.

iPhone as hard drive

At the time of its launch in June 2007, one thing the iPhone could not do, much to the annoyance of pundits and punters alike, was be used as a hard drive to transfer files between computers. This has been a feature of iPods for years, and it's very useful too – for moving documents between work and home, say, for backing up key documents, or for carrying full-resolution photos to share with friends.

There are rumours that Apple may bless the iPhone with a Disk Mode in future software updates. In the meantime, Mac users – though currently not PC users – have a semi-satisfactory solution in the form of Ecamm's iPhoneDrive. Once installed on your Mac, you can use it to drag and drop files on and off your phone.

The problem is that you need to have the application installed on each computer with which you want to use your phone as a drive. This makes it a non-starter for many office computers where the administrators won't allow non-approved, untested software.

iPhoneDrive costs $10 for multiple Macs, though a free demo version is available.

iPhoneDrive ecamm.com/mac/iphonedrive

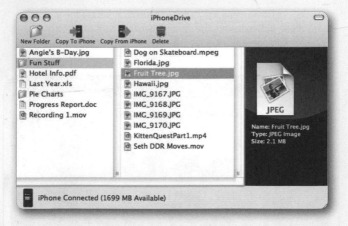

▶ **Most Viewed** The clips most seen by YouTube viewers, not just by you.

▶ **Bookmarks** To start building your bookmarks list, tap the ⊚ button next to a clip and then tap Bookmark.

▶ **Most Recent** The clips most recently submitted to YouTube.

▶ **Top Rated** The clips most highly rated by YouTube users. The iPhone does not let you add your own ratings; you need to go to YouTube.com on a Mac or PC to do that.

▶ **History** The clips you have recently viewed.

Playing clips

Tap any clip to set it playing. The controls work just as with any other video (see p.163).

> TIP: To email a clip's link to a friend, either tap the ⊚ button next to the clip and then tap Share, or, when a video is playing, tap ⊠.

iPhonology

Accessories

plug and play

There are scores of iPhone accessories available, from FM transmitters to travel speakers. The following pages show some of the most useful and desirable add-ons out there, but new ones come out all the time, so keep an eye on iPhone news sites (see p.232) and the Apple Store's iPhone department. When it comes to purchasing, some accessories can be bought on the high street, but for the best selection and prices look online. Compare the offerings of the Apple Store, Amazon, eBay and others, or go straight to the manufacturers, some of which sell direct. Before buying any accessory, make sure it is definitely compatible with the iPhone. Some, but certainly not all, accessories designed for the iPod will work with an iPhone.

Headphone adapters

Models include: **Belkin iPhone adapter; Griffin iPhone adapter**
Cost (approx): $10–15

One common gripe with the iPhone (for a list of others, see p.13) is the fact that the recess which houses
the headphone socket is too small to accept many
standard jacks, leaving you tied to the supplied stereo
Apple headset, or one of the few alternatives that have
appeared, such as those described on p.216. So if you
spent money on a quality pair of earphones for use with
an iPod or other device, they probably won't fit without some sort
of adapter.

   Adapters are relatively inexpensive, but not ideal, as they can
add considerable length to the iPhone and feel cumbersome in
your pocket. Of the brands tested, the Belkin model (pictured
top-right) is relatively small, but not very flexible, while Griffin's
iPhone Adapter (below) offers flex and comes in black or white,
but leaves your iPhone looking like a futuristic sink-plunger.

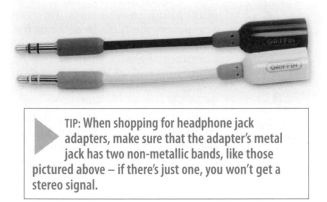

> ▶ **TIP: When shopping for headphone jack
> adapters, make sure that the adapter's metal
> jack has two non-metallic bands, like those
> pictured above – if there's just one, you won't get a
> stereo signal.**

Headphone splitter

Models include: **splitters by Monster and others**
Cost (approx): $10

Headphone splitters allow you to connect two pairs of headphones to a single iPhone (or, indeed, to an iPod or other device). There are many models on the market, but Monster's is one of the few that actually fit the iPhone's recessed jack socket.

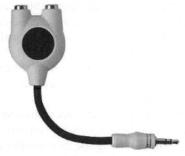

TTY adapters

Models include: **Apple iPhone TTY Adapter**
Cost (approx): $19

Like many other modern phones, the iPhone is compatible with teletypewriters (TTYs), used by the deaf and hard of hearing to communicate via telephone. However, this adatper is required to connect such devices.

Also refered to as TDDs (Telecommunications Devices for the Deaf), TTYs work by using an electronic display that offers one or two lines of text at a time. Both callers need a TTY machine for the communication to work.

Wired headsets

Models include: **Rivet Mobile Stereo Headset; V-MODA Vibe Duo**
Cost (approx): $30–100

The stereo headset that comes bundled with the iPhone is functional enough, but not ideal. Even if the audio quality was better, it still wouldn't be especially comfortable to wear. Many people can't even get the earphones to stay in place.

Thankfully, there are numerous alternatives out there, which are comfortable, "noise isolating" (ie they snugly fill your ear, thereby blocking out ambient noise) and have a minijack plug svelte enough for the iPhone's recessed port. The best budget option is Rivet's Stereo Headset ($30), pictured top right, which offers superior sound, lanyard-style cords, a decent mic and a choice of interchangeable ear buds.

If you're serious about sound quality, you might prefer the V-MODA Vibe Duo (bottom right). These cost $100 but offer crisper, clearer sound, perhaps thanks to their so-called BLISS noise-cancelling system.

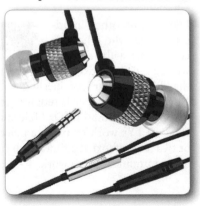

Bluetooth headsets

Models include: **Apple iPhone Bluetooth Headset; Aliph Jawbone**
Cost (approx): $50–130

Bluetooth headsets let you receive calls without getting out your phone or wearing a wired headset. They sit in or around your ear, respond to voice commands and communicate with your phone via radio waves. The main problem is that they can make you appear to be talking to yourself – so expect some strange looks in the street.

Apple's own offering, released at the same time as the iPhone, is unusually small and retails for $130. Though some commentators have pointed out that it bears a striking resemblance to a hash pipe, it scores extra points for coming bundled with a stylish Dual Dock (pictured) for charging the phone and headset simultaneously.

Another slick-looking and pricy option is the Aliph Jawbone ($120). Its over-the-ear clip is very comfortable and it boasts some clever built-in software that adjusts the volume to account for the noise of your environment.

If you're on a tighter budget, most other Bluetooth headsets should work fine. They start at around $50, though the very cheapest ones tend to suffer from poor battery life.

Cases and screen protectors

Models include: **Pacific Rim InvisiShield & iShield; iGone Silicone Skin; Belkin Sports Armband; Incipio Bikini Case; Miniot iWood**
Cost (approx): $15–50

The iPhone is more resistant to scratches and other day-to-day wear than the iPod and many other smart phones. But it's not invulnerable, so you might want to protect yours with some kind of case.

One problem with cases is that they're unlikely to do much for the look of the device, so you might opt instead for an invisible screen protector such as the iPhone InvisiShield, pictured right ($15 for a pack of two, from pacrimtechnologies.com).

For protection of the entire body of the device, you could combine a screen-guard with a slip case such as the colourful Silicone Skin case from iGone ($13 from igonemobile.com) or Pacific Rim's iShield, pictured left, which comes in various colours with a synthetic, leather-ish finish and sells for $35.

If you want to use your iPhone when jogging, or in the gym, look for something with an armband (such as Belkin's Sports Armband, pictured right) or a belt clip.

As with iPods, it didn't take long for more unusual iPhone cases to emerge. These range from the Kharki Bikini Case, pictured bottom left ($20 from myincipio.com), to the hand-carved Miniot iWood, picture bottom right (price yet to be confirmed, from miniot.com).

Some users have pointed out that, since the iPhone gets quite hot, wrapping it in anything that stops the dissipation of heat might cause damage to its internal components. But that seems unlikely – and certainly offset by the reduced risk of damage by dropping.

iPhone speaker units

Models include: **SoundDock by Bose; Logic3 IP104 Speakers; Apple Hi-Fi**
Cost (approx): $50–350

An alternative to connecting your iPhone to a hi-fi or powered speakers (see opposite) is a self-contained speaker system. These are easy to move from room to room (or indeed, from place to place when travelling) and they're space efficient too. A long-standing favourite with iPod owners is the Bose SoundDock, which is also compatible with the iPhone. At $300, it's not cheap, but the sound is exceptionally clear and punchy for the size.

Apple's own home-speaker unit, the Apple Hi-Fi, costs even more (in the US at least), but offers a line input so you can hook up a CD or DVD player, AirPort Express or any other audio device. And if you don't mind buying enough batteries to power a small village, it can be taken out and about ghettoblaster-style. It works fine with the iPhone, but you will need to get hold of an iPhone Universal Dock adapter to plug in.

There are many smaller, less expensive systems available. One example is the Logic3 IP104, which can hold the iPhone in either portrait or landscape mode.

Powered speakers

Models include: **Audioengine 5; Genelec 8030A**
Cost (approx): **$350–1200**

One problem with the iPhone speaker units described opposite is that they offer no flexibility in terms of stereo separation – unlike traditional hi-fi speakers, which you can position as far apart as you like. Pairs of powered speakers – aka active speakers – get around this problem. One or both of the speakers contains its own amplifier, so all you need is a sound source – such as an iPhone or your computer.

The Audioengine 5 stands out as a very neat solution for both iPhones and iPods (pictured here with an iPod dock connected). These 70W-per-channel speakers feature a USB port up-top for charging and a separate minijack socket for the audio. For the price ($250/£200), they sound excellent.

At the top end of the market are Genelec's range of bi-amplified speakers (ie both speakers have an integrated amplifier). These have long been a popular choice for studio use, thanks to their incredibly detailed and rich sound, but they're equally well suited for audiophile home use. Each speaker connects using its own XLR cable, so you'll have to get a suitable two-channel preamp or DI box to create a "balanced" signal from your iPhone. The resulting sound is hugely impressive.

221

Hi-fi and speaker connectors

Models include: **Belkin Stereo Link Cables**
Cost (approx): $10–15

Whether you want to connect your stereo to your computer to digitize your vinyl collection (see p.126), or connect your iPhone to your hi-fi to play music in your living room, you'll probably need an RCA-to-minijack cable – also known as an RCA-to-3.5mm cable. These are very easy to find, though many won't fit into the iPhone's recessed headphone socket without an adapter.

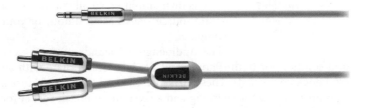

One example that will fit is the one made by Belkin, which also happens to come in an iPhone-friendly grey-silver colour scheme.

Belkin also produce a matching minijack-to-minijack cable, which can be useful for connecting your iPhone to line-in sockets on computers and speakers.

AirTunes

Models include: **Apple AirPort Express**
Cost (approx): **$79**

Many people connect an iPhone or iPod to their hi-fi for home listening. But if you have a laptop, it's often more convenient to play music direct from iTunes. Aside from anything else, there's room for a bigger music collection on your computer than on your iPhone.

If your hi-fi has a line-in socket, you can hook up your laptop with an RCA-to-minijack cable (see opposite), but a neater solution is Apple's AirPort Express wireless base station, with its so-called AirTunes feature. Attach one of these to a power point near to your hi-fi and connect it to the stereo with an RCA-to-minijack cable. Then any computer with Wi-Fi can beam music straight from iTunes to the hi-fi.

AirPort Express can also act as a wireless router for Internet and printer sharing.

Given that the iPhone has Wi-Fi, you'd hope that, like a Mac or PC, it could stream music wirelessly to an AirPort Express. It remains to be seen whether this capability will be added to the phone in future software upgrades.

FM radio transmitters

Models include: **Griffin iTrip**
Cost (approx): $40 (not available in the UK)

This clever little device will turn your iPhone into an extremely short-range FM radio station. Once you've attached it, any radio within range (theoretically around thirty feet, though a few feet is more realistic to achieve a decent quality of sound) can then tune in to whatever music or podcast the iPhone is playing. The sound quality isn't as good as you'd get by attaching to a stereo via a cable (see previous page) and there can be interference, especially in built-up areas. But FM transmitters are very convenient and allow you to play your iPhone's music through any radio, including those – such as portables and car stereos – which don't offer a line-in socket.

Some models, such as the Griffin iTrip (pictured), which will soon be available for the iPhone, connect directly to the Dock socket and draw power from the phone's battery. Others contain their own battery and connect via the headphone jack – not as neat, but these types will work with any audio device.

FM transmitters are currently legal in North America but not in the UK, where they breach radio transmission laws. This hasn't stopped many Brits importing them from the States, however.

Car accessories

Several major car manufacturers are now offering built-in iPod/iPhone connectivity – among them BMW, Volvo, Mercedes and Nissan – which will allow you to control your music from your dashboard. Combine with a Bluetooth headset for safely receiving calls (see p.217) and you're all kitted out. But don't worry if you lack a recent high-end vehicle – you can also do things piecemeal:

Audio connectors

Unless your car stereo has a line-in socket, the two options are an FM transmitter (see opposite) or a cassette adapter. The latter will only work with a cassette player, of course, but they tend to provide better sound than an FM transmitter, and they're not expensive. There are various cassette adapters on the market, but the very cheapest ones have a tendency to produce wails and hisses. The Monster iCarPlay ($25) is one model that's both decent quality and compatible with the iPhone's recessed minijack socket.

Chargers

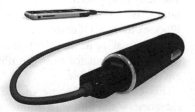

For in-car charging, try an XtremeMac's InCharge Auto Charger (pictured) or the Griffin PowerJolt Charger, both of which slot into standard 12v car accessory socket.

For more auto iPhone solutions, visit iplaymycar.com

Websites

Online apps & iPhone supersites

There are two categories of iPhone website. The first includes sites focusing on the iPhone itself, with news, reviews, troubleshooting advice, forums and the like. The second includes any site that has been specially designed to fit perfectly on the iPhone's screen, without the need for zooming in and out.

Many sites in the latter category are interactive tools designed to do one thing, from calculating tips at restaurants to playing chess. Such sites are often referred to as apps, applications or widgets, and they're appearing thick and fast, not least because building interactive websites is the only way programmers can add to the iPhone's toolkit. Of course, most programmers would prefer to be making "real" apps that sit on the Home screen along with Apple's own widgets, but for now the iPhone remains a closed platform and this isn't possible.

This chapter lists some of the best iPhone websites in both categories – starting with online applications and continuing with sites focusing on the device itself.

Directories

There are several websites that offer directories of iPhone-optimized websites and apps, arranged into categories. These can be useful to locate tools when you're out and about, or just fun to browse. Some are laid out like traditional directories…

iLounge ilounge.com/index.php/mobile/iphonecats
iphondo iphondo.com
iPhone Apps Manager iphoneappsmanager.com

…while others are essentially blogs which review new apps and arrange their previous posts by application category:

AppleiPhoneHome appleiphonehome.com
iPhone Application List iphoneapplicationlist.com
iPhoneSource iphonesource.org
iPhoneWidgetlist iphonewidgetlist.com

Best of all, however, are those which simulate the iPhone Home screen, making themselves seem like an integral part of the iPhone software…

AppMarks appmarks.com
Leaflets getleaflets.com

The above let you customize the homepage of the site, so that your favourite apps are never more than a click away. And, in the case of AppMarks, each link opens in a new window, so the homepage stays available in the background. Of course, you could instead just assemble a list of your favourite online apps within your bookmarks (see p.174). But it's not as nice-looking or convenient.

Games

Though you won't be Tomb Raiding with Ms Croft anytime soon on the iPhone, there are many fun and addictive online games at your disposal. Alongside classics such as…

Chess shredderchess.com/iphone
Matching Pairs digiwidge.com/
   i-tiles/i-tiles.html
Poker iphone.scenario.com
Sudoku sudoku.myiphone.pl

… you'll find less familiar gems such as Diametry (where you connect lines of shapes) and iTouch (where you chase dots around the screen with your fingers).

iTouch widgetaria.com
Diametry diamenty.myiphone.pl
Wordbreaker wordbreaker.org

> **TIP:** If you have your own website and you want to create an iPhone-friendly version, you'll find advice for adapting your pages at developer.apple.com/iphone and barcamp.org/iPhoneDevCamp

Useful tools for when out & about

The following miscellany of useful online apps should give you the idea of the kinds of things that are out there. As for the rest, if you can imagine it, it probably exists, so Google it.

Tips and tricks

If your mental arithmetic suffers after a couple of glasses of wine, turn to the following to help you split the cost of the meal you just ate and work out an appropriate tip.

I Can Has Tip? iphonetipper.com
TipCalc dannyg.com/iphone/tipCalc

In case you're thinking of driving home, tap in what you've consumed, when, and your weight, and see that you're in no fit state.

Blood Alcohol Turbowidget bac.turbowidget.com

Cheap gas

Tap in your zip code (US-only at present) and find the best-value fuel in your vicinity.

GasApp gasapp.com/new.html

Wikkid notes

Technically minded and tired of the iPhone's limited Notes tool? Set up your own quick-loading, iPhone-optimized wiki.

A Little Wiki stevenf.com/2007/07/w2_a_little_wiki.php

iPhone Periodic Table of Elements

You're out and about and you see an atom that's unfamiliar … where do you turn?

Periodic Table code.jalenack.com/periodic

Mobile versions of regular sites

Many popular websites offer a version for browsing on mobile devices in general or iPhones specifically. These not only fit nicely on small screens but also load much faster, since they come without the large graphics and other bells and whistles.

Sometimes, if the server recognizes that you're using a mobile Web browser, the mobile version of a site will appear automatically. At other times, you'll have to navigate to the mobile version manually – look for a link on the homepage.

Mobile sites often have the same address but with "m", "mobile" or "iphone" after a slash or in place of the "www". For example, among the A-listers:

Digg digg.com/iphone
eBay mobile.ebay.co.uk
Facebook m.facebook.com
Flickr m.flickr.com

And the B-listers…

101 Cookbooks 101cookbooks.com/iphonerecipes
BrainyQuote brainyquote.com/iphone.html
This Day in History mackiev.com/iphone

If a site doesn't feature a mobile version, that doesn't mean it doesn't exist. Thanks to RSS newsfeeds, Web designers can easily create iPhone-optimized pages of content from sites they don't control. For example, iActu serves up headlines (with links) from the *New York Times*, *USA Today* and other major US newspapers, while Pocket Tweets lets you find out what Twitterers around the world are doing right now.

iActu widgetinfo.net/iphone
Pocket Tweets pockettweets.com

Online address books

Really useful … a means of looking up people's numbers without having to waste minutes on calls to directory enquiries. At the time of writing, only iPhone People Finder has been optimized for the iPhone, but the others are still worth bookmarking, and both Yellow Pages sites work well in landscape mode.

UK

192.com (UK) 192.com
Directory Enquiries (UK) bt.com/directory-enquiries
Yellow Pages (UK) yell.com

US

iPhone People Finder (US) 2robots.com/iphone
Yellow Pages (US) yellowpages.com

Sites about the iPhone

Within weeks of the iPhone's launch there were already scores of websites focusing on nothing else. Of course, all the existing iPod sites were also enjoying the new gadget. Such sites are packed with tips, troubleshooting advice, accessory reviews and forums where you can post queries. Following are some of the best.

News, reviews and how-tos

Everything iPhone everythingiphone.com
iLounge ilounge.com
iPhone Atlas iphoneatlas.com
iPhone Freak iphonefreak.com

Accessory stores

Amazon amazon.com **or** .co.uk
Apple Store apple.com/store
Griffin griffintechnology.com
iLounge iLounge.com/loungestore.php

Help

If you have an ailing iPhone or you want the latest tip, tap Safari and drop in to one of these support sites…

Apple Support apple.com/support/iphone
iPhone Atlas iphoneatlas.com
MacFixit macfixit.com

… or pose a question to one of the iPhone junkies who spend their waking hours on forums such as:

Apple Forums discussions.apple.com
Everything iPhone everythingiphone.com/forum

iLounge forums forums.ilounge.com
iPhone Forum iphoneforum.info
MacRumors forums.macrumors.com
Talk iPhone talkiphone.com

There's even a dedicated iPhone social networking site, though it remains to be seen if it will really take off:

iPhone Colony iphonecolony.com

Hacks and mods

If you're the kind of person who likes to take things apart, check out the "Cracking Open the Apple iPhone" article at TechRepublic, and follow up with one of the numerous "iPhone disassembly" or "iPhone mod" posts on YouTube and Flickr. Trying any such thing at home will, of course, thoroughly void your warranty.

TechRepublic techrepublic.com
Flickr flickr.com
YouTube youtube.com

And to find out who's recently managed to get an iPhone to do what, drop in to:

iPhone Hacks iphonehacks.com

Scripts and plug-ins
Apple Downloads apple.com/downloads
Doug's AppleScripts dougscripts.com/itunes
iLounge ilounge.com/downloads.php

Blogs

Add the following to your RSS page (see p.176) for an endless drop-feed of Apple titbits – including plenty on the iPhone.

Daring Fireball daringfireball.com
iPhone News iphonews.com
Macalope macalope.com
Secret Diary of Steve Jobs fakesteve.blogspot.com
Tao of Mac the.taoofmac.com
The iPhone Blog theiphoneblog.com

Feedback

If you have a suggestion about how the iPhone could be improved, then tell Apple at:

iPhone Feedback apple.com/feedback/iphone.html

18

iPhone weirdness

Staggering strangeness

It is, without a doubt, a weird world, and there's nothing quite like a new Apple gadget to bring the crackpots out of the cupboard. Even before anyone had seen an iPhone, the Web was alive with crazy predictions; then there were the much-publicized queues in New York City in the days before the launch; and since then it has only got odder. What follows are a few dispatches from the dark world of iPhone obsession…

The predictions

There was no shortage of ideas online for what the iPhone would look like, ranging from the nearly sane…

baekdal.com

Isamu Sanada

idgugu@empal.com

Ministry of Tech-

236

… to the completely insane. For more, see:

Product Dose productdose.com/article.php?article_id=5893
iPhone Concept Blog appleiphone.blogspot.com

There were even a few ideas that did more for the evolution of the rubber band and sticky tape than either iPods or phones…

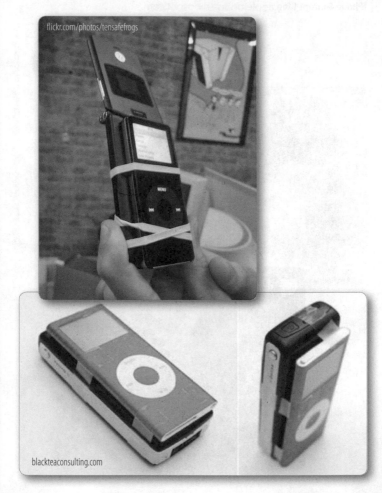

The Apple phone that never was

Perhaps the strangest images to have circulated the Web, however, are those illustrated below. Allegedly, they illustrate a phone for which Apple filed a patent back in 1982…

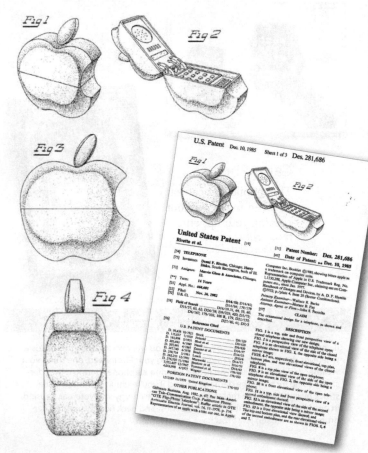

Wool iPhone

The iPhone for minors and knitwear fanatics:
daddytypes.com

Cake iPhone

The mobile you can eat between meals without ruining your appetite:
mobilewhack.com/
iphone-cake---cool

Lightning warning!

If your iPhone obsession is so severe that you wear your earbuds or headset whatever the weather, you might be risking your life. Indeed, one thing your weather widget won't tell you is that wearing earphones during a thunderstorm could increase the damage caused if you're unlucky enough to be struck by lightning. The metal can channel the energy into your ear, causing, in one instance, "… wishbone-shaped chest and neck burns, ruptured eardrums and a broken jaw". You have been warned.

Cotton and silk

If your desire for an iPhone isn't matched by your bank balance, tide yourself over with a paper version, courtesy of: homepage.mac.com/colin-baxter/ipod/ipodclick.html

If money *isn't* an issue, on the other hand… gizmodo.com/gadgets/igems

iPhone shuffle

There are several incarnations of this theme doing the rounds ... a screenless phone whose USP is its ability to call and text your friends and family at random.
blog.thesedays.com

iPhone generator

Worried about your iPhone's battery life-span? You could take the advice on p.69, or just plonk for an iPhone generator for power emergencies. Watch this space for the hotly anticipated hydro-electric version (dam not supplied): andrewsavory.com

iPhone size

An essential reference tool if you ever need to communicate the size of your iPhone to a stranger but do not happen to have said digital gizmo to hand: iphonesize.com

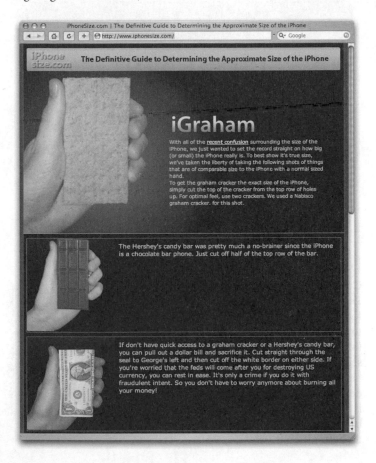

Engraving

Apple have not yet offered an engraving service for the iPhone, but the guys at DeviceNineSix.com have…

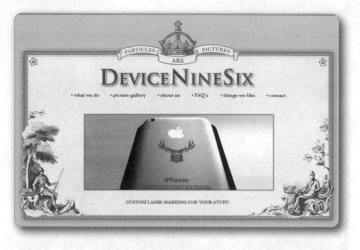

Lego iPhones

Compared to the wondrous Lego creations that can be found online paying tribute to the humble iPod, those for the iPhone are rather second-rate. Admittedly it is hard to create a flat-screened device using a medium that is so fundamentally knob-bly, but surely someone can do better than this?

flickr.com/photos/gilest

YouTube

Thankfully, there's more iPhone (and Lego) nonsense on YouTube to keep us all entertained. The "2001: A Space iPhone" and "Conan iPhone Commercial" clips are both essential viewing…

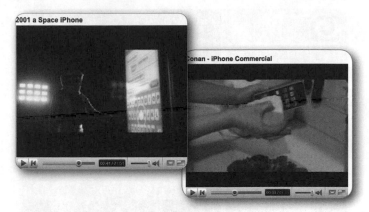

…and these animations are guaranteed to raise a smile:

Will It Blend?

Who on Earth would want to use an iPhone as an iPhone when there's the option of turning it into a smoothie instead?

willitblend.com

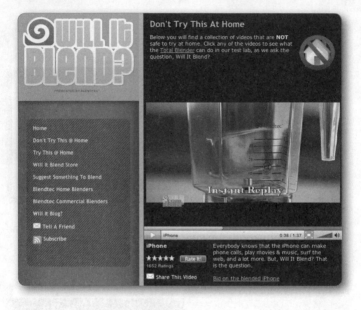

Index

index

index